Maybe You Should Give Up

MAYBE YOU SHOULD GIVE UP

7 WAYS TO GET OUT OF YOUR OWN WAY AND TAKE CONTROL OF YOUR LIFE

BYRON MORRISON

NEW YORK

LONDON • NASHVILLE • MELBOURNE • VANCOUVER

MAYBE **YOU** SHOULD **GIVE UP**

7 WAYS TO GET OUT OF YOUR OWN WAY AND TAKE CONTROL OF YOUR LIFE

Published in New York, New York, by Morgan James Publishing. Morgan James is a trademark of Morgan James, LLC. www.MorganJamesPublishing.com

Proudly distributed by Ingram Publisher Services.

Morgan James BOGO™

A **FREE** ebook edition is available for you or a friend with the purchase of this print book.

CLEARLY SIGN YOUR NAME ABOVE

Instructions to claim your free ebook edition:
1. Visit MorganJamesBOGO.com
2. Sign your name CLEARLY in the space above
3. Complete the form and submit a photo of this entire page
4. You or your friend can download the ebook to your preferred device

ISBN 9781636980645 paperback
ISBN 9781636980652 ebook
Library of Congress Control Number:
2022946016

Cover and Interior Design by:
Chris Treccani
www.3dogcreative.net

Morgan James is a proud partner of Habitat for Humanity Peninsula and Greater Williamsburg. Partners in building since 2006.

Get involved today! Visit: www.morgan-james-publishing.com/giving-back

AUTHOR'S NOTE

Throughout this book, I share real-world examples from my private clients to help you better understand certain challenges, along with how you can implement changes in your own life. While the stories are factual, for confidentiality reasons, all of the names have been changed.

To help you on this journey, I've also put together a few bonuses, including a video series on how to take control of your life, a community to keep you accountable and various other resources.

Download them for free at:

www.byronmorrison.com/bonuses

CONTENTS

INTRODUCTION

Have you noticed that every self-help book is the same these days?

Think about it.

Pretty much every one of them gives you some iteration of the following process:

1. Figure out where you are and what's broken, painful, or problematic about being there. Maybe you're over-weight, overwhelmed, overworked, or under your potential (or all four!)
2. Decide on where you want to be instead. (Thin, relaxed, rich, attractive, etc.)
3. Figure out what you need to do to get from where you are now to where you want to be. (Usually by following the plan, strategy or instructions taught by whoever wrote the book or designed the program.)
4. Do those things for as long as it takes to get results.
5. Ride off into the sunset with the amazing body, mind, career, and/or relationship you've always wanted.

Seems simple, right? There's just one problem: it doesn't work. Not long-term anyway.

This is why despite their best intentions, most people who try to follow these processes never actually make progress. Sure, they get excited at first, thinking this course, book or challenge will skyrocket them to success. Yet before long, that motivational spark wears off and the real work begins. And then what happens? They lose that initial momentum, stagnate and become discouraged...at least until they discover the next course, book, or challenge that gets them excited again.

Raise your hand if that sounds familiar. You can't see me, but I definitely have my hand up. And I bet you have, too. It's exhausting, isn't it? But why do we do this? Why do we get trapped in this unending cycle of excitement and dejection? Why do we continuously fall short of the Instagram-worthy results that the gurus tell us we'll get, if we just do what they tell us to? Why do we fail over and over again at keeping off the weight, earning more money or building a deeper relationship? Most gurus will say this happens because we didn't hustle hard enough, didn't put in the work or didn't want it badly enough. And sometimes that's true...but most of the time, it's totally wrong. That scapegoating idea comes from *them* trying to make *their* programs sound like universal solutions that work for absolutely everyone—and to discredit anyone who might claim otherwise.

Want to know the real reason? *We do it to ourselves.* We get in our own way and sabotage our efforts. To be clear, self-sabotage isn't the same as just not working hard enough or not wanting it badly enough. Most of the people I talk to who struggle with self-sabotage are hard workers who really want to change their lives. Often, they even get really close to achieving their goals and desires. Yet somehow, they seem to always fall short of the life they could be living. They don't mean to do it. They don't try to do it. They sometimes don't even know they're doing it. But they do it anyway. And then, to make things even worse, they get back up and try the same things again. And guess what happens? They just end up getting in their own way again.

Raise your hand one more time if this sounds frustratingly familiar. In case you haven't already guessed, my hand is up again.

My own worst enemy

Back in 2014, I reached a point in my life where I felt stuck. I was overweight, burnt out and felt trapped in a job that was killing me. Every day became a battle just to get through. To cope with what was going on, I'd spend my weekends intoxicated, on a diet of Jack Daniels and KFC to numb how I felt. And it wasn't that I didn't want to change or do something about my situation. I had huge goals and dreams. I wanted to do something that mattered, to help other people, to feel like I was doing more than surviving the day. Yet despite that, I was my own worst enemy, sabotaging everything from my relationships to my health, my professional success and my happiness. The worst part was that I knew exactly what I needed to do to turn things around. But instead of doing those things, I'd procrastinate, lose motivation, or avoid the very actions that would get me out of the hole that I was in. Like when I'd delay launching my business because everything wasn't *"perfect"*. I'd ruin a relationship as my own internal barriers would stop me from letting someone else in. Or I'd mess up all my progress on a diet by going on an all-out binge. Truth be told, I felt lost and deflated, to the point where I became so depressed I didn't even want to leave the house.

At this point, most gurus would talk about a life-changing occurrence that snapped them out of their downward spiral. Maybe they lost a loved one, went bankrupt, got divorced, or suffered a debilitating illness. Problem was, I'd already had one of those wake-up calls, and I was still asleep. A few years prior, my dad's cancer showed me how quickly life can turn upside down. During his treatment, he had most of his bowel surgically removed and he spent 25 days in ICU, most of that on life support and breathing through a tracheostomy. That for me was the wake-up call that I needed to change, as I realized how much time I'd wasted that I could never get back. Yet despite that and my newfound desire to turn my life around, I seemed to still be able to find a way to mess things up. It was so frustrating, as I knew exactly what I needed to do. But instead, I felt like I was going around in circles, where I'd make some changes, then quickly stop or quit at the first sign of failure. So even though I had great intentions, for the next few years I barely made any progress. Eventually, it hit me: I couldn't keep trying the same things hoping that change would happen for me. So, I gave up.

Now before you panic, let me be clear: I didn't give up on my life, my goals, my dreams, or my desire to change how things were going for me. I didn't accept a life of mediocrity, lying on the couch eating Doritos, or throwing in the towel and collapsing in a ditch.

But I did give up on playing it safe.

I gave up on being afraid of failure.

I gave up on worrying about what other people thought about me.

I gave up on trying to be perfect.

I gave up on all my excuses about why I couldn't succeed.

I gave up putting off my happiness.

And here's the crazy thing: it worked. By giving up on those things, I was finally able to turn my life around. Several years later, I've kept off the weight, my relationships are stronger and more connected than ever, and I'm no longer just battling to get through the day. I've also built a business that fulfills me emotionally and financially, written multiple bestselling books, and for the first time, I can truly say I'm happy. On that journey, I've been fortunate to work with clients from around the world, which has allowed me to gain unique insights and perspectives into the challenges people face and how to overcome them. This experience, combined with over a decade's worth of research, has allowed me to discover what it really takes to help someone reach their potential. And now I want to take what I learned and pass it on to you, so that you too can get out of your own way and take back control of your life.

All of which brings me to the title of this book.

Maybe you should give up.

Not on the life you want or the dreams you've had for years. But instead, maybe you should give up on the things that are actually holding you back from them. *Maybe you should give up on anything that is getting in the way of you living the life that you want.*

If that sounds really simple, that's because it is. But just because it's simple, doesn't mean it's easy. After all, you may need to give up on things that you've been holding onto for most of your life. And we'll talk more about what those things could be in just a moment. But before you even address what you need to give up *on*, you need to be okay with the idea of giving up *at all*. And there are two sides to that: an internal side and an external side.

Why you don't want to give up

The biggest *internal* struggle around giving up is realizing that you're already fighting yourself. Your mind is programmed in a way that it wants to keep you doing the things you're already doing. This default way of operating can be traced back to the start of human existence. Just think of the days of the cavemen, where everything was all about survival. Back then a good day would mean finding some shelter, scavenging some food and not getting eaten by a wild animal. Even though society has evolved a lot since then, your brain has evolved *much slower*. Sure, it has a lot of higher-level functions now, but its baseline programming is the same, and its primary focus is still to keep you alive at all costs. In other words, your mind is programmed to prioritize *survival*, not happiness, progress, joy or success.

Because of that, whenever you try to do something new— even something you know will help you be more successful, happy or reach your goals—your brain reacts by essentially screaming *"Don't do that! Stay where you are!"* Even though you may be unhappy with what's going on in your life, your brain takes comfort in what it knows. After all, you've survived everything you've been through, regardless of how challenging it was or how it made you feel. By this logic, what you have now is far safer than anything new could ever be.

This explains why when you try to put yourself out there or let go of something familiar, your brain tells you that it won't work. The timing isn't right. You're not ready yet. You won't be as good as everyone else. It's also why, as soon as you hit your first failures or struggles, your brain jumps straight to telling you that you couldn't do it. That it's too hard. People are laughing at you. Or maybe things weren't so bad before after all.

In other words, you sabotage yourself—because your brain wants you to keep everything the same. The same kinds of relationships. The same amount of weight on your body. The same amount of wealth. The same amount of happiness, joy and success. No matter how much *you* want those things to change, your brain sees those changes as threats, and it will do everything in its power to talk you out of them. And as we'll see in a second here, it does that by making you want to cling to comfortable, familiar thoughts and beliefs that feel safe but keep you stuck. This is why you are never going to be able to live the life that you want until you give up on the way you think. Because until you do that, your brain will keep filling your head with negative and limiting thoughts, all in a desperate attempt to keep you where you are.

Why no one else wants you to give up, either

The biggest *external* problem with giving up is that the idea itself is almost universally demonized and looked down upon. Especially with all the motivational fluff of "keep pushing," "never quit," and "hustle harder" spouted out all over your newsfeed. This has all created a perception that giving up is failing, bailing or copping out. It's admitting defeat in a world where if you're not a winner, you're nothing. All of this further reinforces that subconscious fear that doing something different or changing direction will draw criticism from everyone around you. Because what will they think if you change your mind on something you said you wanted, or you've spent years working for? That potential judgment alone can be enough to cause you to accept how things are.

I know this was why I stayed in a job that was destroying me, as I felt like having a full-time corporate position was expected by my friends, family and colleagues. Worse, when I told some friends I wanted to launch a business, they told me it would never work and that I was *crazy*. And I know I'm not alone. I've spoken to countless people who are in careers they hate, but they won't change paths because of what other people will say and think. Just the thought of that change triggers a huge internal battle, where we seem to convince ourselves that staying unhappy is better than having to face other people's opinions that we are going backward.

The truth is that a lot of people like you just where you are. If you don't give up on the things holding *you* back, then they don't have to face their own unwillingness to give up on the things holding *them* back. By encouraging you to sacrifice your growth, dreams and the life you really want, they get to feel better about themselves and how disappointing their life has turned out. Even though they may not consciously, intentionally or maliciously be doing this, it's in their best interest to talk you out of giving up. Like that friend who when you're on a diet, says *"just have one cookie, it won't hurt"* or *"just live a little"*. They don't understand your desire to change because they don't have any desire to change themselves (or if they do, they see it as doomed before it even begins). Plus, misery loves company, which is why it's easier to accept their own lot in life or to justify their actions if you're stuck down there with them.

The external side of giving up is made even harder by all of the self-help gurus preaching to *never* give up...because if you give up, the thing you give up on might be working with them! Trust me, no matter how much they say they want you to succeed, most of them will never tell you to do anything that stops you from paying them. At the end of the day, you succeeding is bad for business. They want you to get results long enough to convince you that it works, but not long enough that it leads to lasting changes. So when you fall off track, you'll blame yourself, coming back eager and ready for what they launch next.

I'm not even making that up to make other coaches and trainers look bad—I wish I could say I was! The truth is that I have been taught this technique. During my fitness qualifications, we were told to use confusing or complex exercises that clients need our help with and can't do on their own. By including movements that require two people, you build a feeling of dependency where they become reliant on you, convincing them they can't make progress by themselves. It's the perfect strategy to keep clients coming back month after month. This is a big part of how coaches, consultants and trainers—the gurus I've been talking about—make a lot of their money: by making their clients keep coming back, even when what they're teaching may not be optimal or even helpful anymore.

I'm going to get personal for a second here: I really, really hate that approach. It's unethical, it's unhelpful, it's the textbook definition of overpromising and underdelivering, and it just feels *wrong* to me. So I decided a long time ago I would never work that way. Even if it meant losing money in the short run. That's why my approach has always been about sustainability. I believe it's important to guide and set you up in a way that teaches you to do things on your own, without needing me or more of my help past a certain point. Sure, there are situations where people enjoy the accountability and thrive on the extra support, which is why I do have clients who have been with me for multiple years. But they are there because it helps them continue to grow, not because it's something they depend on or because they'll fall off track without me.

The way I see it is that anyone can get results for 90 days, but the testament that it's worked is that you're still sticking to it five years from now. Because of that, everything I'll be sharing with you is focused on how you can make lasting changes in your life. So, in case you're worried that I might turn out to be one of the gurus I've been ranting about...I hope that sets your mind at rest.

The secret no one tells you about giving up

Here's the real secret that the gurus don't know and will never tell you: giving up is actually the key to being successful.

Most people use Thomas Edison as an example of innovation or perseverance, and he's definitely an example of both those qualities. But there's something else he did really well: he gave up. You've no doubt heard the famous quote of his where he stated that "I have not failed 10,000 times—I've successfully found 10,000 ways that will not work". In other words, he gave up on 10,000 other approaches he took until he found the one that worked.

Or take Elon Musk. Regardless of what you may think of him as a person, his impact on the world is undeniable. Yet throughout his career, he's failed publicly in spectacular fashion—at one point PayPal was voted the worst business concept of the year. Yet rather than quitting, he gave up on the initial idea of PayPal being security software for handheld devices and pivoted it towards becoming the virtual wallet it is today.

In both of these examples, these people could have kept trying the same thing, hoping their initial idea would eventually flourish. But instead, they gave up on everything that wasn't working. They recognized that repeating the same actions and hoping for some miracle that they would result in success was not only short-sighted—it was also never going to get them to where they wanted to be. And they didn't just give up on what they were doing. They also gave up on worrying about the judgment, criticism and limitations of others who told them they were crazy, focusing instead on their goals and what they wanted to achieve. They completely blocked out the world and anything external that took their focus away from where they were going. That's why they finally succeeded.

In reality, every single successful person gives up all of the time. They give up on strategies and approaches that aren't getting results. They give up on ideas or goals they realize they don't want. They give up on negative feelings and fears that hold them back. They give up on anything that is getting in the way of creating the life they want.

Those who stay stuck in self-sabotage though, often do so due to their reluctance to give up on something. Maybe it's their approach to how they do their job, a strategy in their business, a way to try and lose weight, or how they deal with problems. Whatever it is, they repeatedly try the same actions and behaviors, then beat themselves up wondering why they aren't making progress. As I shared with you already, I'm as guilty of this as anyone. For years I was stuck on this hamster wheel, convinced that I just needed to try harder and that next time I'd finally get it right.

You've probably heard that the definition of insanity is doing the same thing over and over hoping for different results. If you truly want to move forward, you need to give up on everything that is holding you back and start doing something different.

But what do I give up on?

I mentioned above that there are specific thought patterns and beliefs your brain pushes you to cling to. Remember, it wants to keep you safe and secure, so this is its defense to get you to stay the same and accept the way things are. That in itself is why, at times, you can find yourself in an internal tug-of-war between what you want and the way the voice in your head tells you that life has to be. Subconsciously, we're holding on to all those other perceived benefits—it's easy, it's familiar, it's yours, it's more time in bed, it's less time learning something new, it comes without the discomfort of facing the unknown.

Think of these beliefs like carrying a bag of rocks on your back, weighing you down in everything that you do and making any kind of growth or change more difficult. The process I'll be taking you through in this book is all about removing those rocks one at a time. By doing so, you'll be able to feel lighter at every turn, until eventually, you take the last rock out and finally feel the lightness of carrying only yourself.

What is holding you back?

In my experience, there are seven major beliefs that people need to give up on in order to achieve the results they want in their lives.

1. Reactiveness: *"I can't control what is happening."*
2. Fear: *"What if I fail? Even worse, what if I succeed?"*
3. Short-term thinking: *"I want comfort now more than I want success later."*
4. The future: *"My goals are so far away, I'm going to take forever to get there."*
5. Comparison: *"Look how great those other people are at this already!"*
6. Self-criticism: *"I'm not doing this right, I should just quit."*
7. Unhappiness: *"It's not the right time to prioritize my happiness, I'll get to it eventually."*

Each of these beliefs is a mental rock that weighs you down and keeps you stuck in its own unique way. But there are two important things to know about them.

First, these beliefs don't exist in isolation. They interrelate with each other, compounding and exacerbating each other's effects. For instance, you might fixate on losing a certain amount of weight as the key to being happy with yourself. But then you get intimidated by the toned, lean people working out in the gym. So, you obsess over counting every calorie for a month and beat yourself up that you're not losing weight quickly enough, and finally, you throw in the towel because you had a bad day and devoured a tub of ice cream. That's unhappiness, comparison, self-criticism and reactiveness all piling onto each other.

Second, these aren't new ideas. You've already heard of all of them, you've no doubt thought about them and read other pieces about them before. You may even know you struggle with some of them. And because they aren't revolutionary ideas, they can be easy to dismiss. That may even have happened already, where you looked at that list and thought to yourself—*"I already know this, what am I supposed to get out of things I already know?"*

Here's the thing about that...if you know something, but you're not doing it, you don't really know it. If you *really knew* how badly clinging to fear, fixating on the future or being too hard on yourself was screwing up your life, then you probably wouldn't allow those beliefs to cause you to get in your own way anymore.

As we go through this book together, I'm going to challenge you to keep an open mind. Perhaps a bit more than you think you might need to. Because here's the thing...even though many of these ideas may not be new, the way I help you approach and overcome them will be. That's why I want you to commit to putting aside what you already think you know and what you've already tried, and instead, view this as a new chapter in your life.

How this book will help you give up

From the work I've done with clients over the last decade, I've seen that to create lasting change, you have to tackle the underlying problem from every angle. So in the context of this book, you must learn to give up *all* of the beliefs that are weighing you down. But that's a lot to deal with at once! I certainly couldn't handle facing all seven of those beliefs at the same time, so I won't ask you to do that either. Instead, this book is designed to handle the weight of one rock at a time. Each chapter will tackle one belief and help you give it up in a healthy, powerful way—and as you give up on each one, in turn, the momentum will create a domino effect, making giving up on the next ones easier.

It's also why the chapters are in the order they are. This journey starts with confronting reactiveness and fear—those are the deepest beliefs, the ones that keep you from getting started and building momentum towards the life you want in the first place. They're the boulders, the biggest rocks that are so heavy that just lifting them is prohibitive. Then you'll face short-term thinking, fixating on the future and comparison with others— the beliefs that are most likely to derail you as you're starting to make progress and facing expected (and unexpected) struggles along the way. These are midsize rocks that fit well enough in your sack but slow you down more and more the longer you carry them. We'll finish by working through self-criticism and unhappiness—the beliefs most likely to sabotage you as you get closer to the life you want. These are the beliefs that can cause you to doubt whether you're on the right path or even if you deserve success to begin with! They're the small pebbles in your shoes that hurt enough to distract you from the beautiful mountaintop view.

For this to effectively work, you need to *read the chapters in order*. There's no point in taking a small pebble out of your shoe if you're struggling under the weight of a giant boulder.

To help you fully understand and implement what I share with you, I'll also share my own stories and real-world examples from working with clients from around the world. This will allow you to see the necessary mindset shifts in action and help you gain clarity on how you can follow through with them yourself. I'll also give you tools, self-reflection questions and exercises to do, to ensure that this won't be just a book you *read*, but a book that actually helps you get results.

Now that we've got all that covered, are you ready to give up?

Then let's get started.

Part 1:

THE BOULDERS

The hardest part of any journey is getting started. Whether you're going on a trek up a mountain, starting to get in shape or trying to get a new business off the ground, the first steps will always be the most challenging. As we talked about a few pages ago, your brain doesn't want you to go on *any* journeys. Journeys can be dangerous! They're full of change, uncertainty and unknowns, making them an inherent risk. This is why instead, your subconscious wants you to stay where you are, where it feels safe.

To stop you from even starting, your brain has dropped two immense boulders to hold you down. These boulders can make it feel like the weight of the world is on your shoulders. And when you're carrying that much weight, how far do you think you are going to get? Not very. Which is exactly what your brain wants for you. It wants you to expend all your effort just thinking about these boulders, to the point that you don't even try to pick them up. When you think about it, it's a pretty good trick—your brain keeps safe by getting you to focus on what's in your way, instead of what you want. This way, even during the times you do try to pick them up, the sheer weight of those boulders causes you to quickly put them back down.

The worst part is that when it happens, they feel even heavier to pick up the next time. So it's far easier to just accept that the challenge is too difficult and you can't move forward. This is why the solution here is to *stop trying to carry the boulders*. Give up on them. Leave them behind. Don't let your brain convince you that you need them. Because you don't.

Here are the two belief boulders you must give up on: the belief that you can't control your own life enough to change it, and the belief that changing your life is too scary to do it. Once you give up on these, you'll feel lighter, more in control and one step closer to where you want to be.

CHAPTER 1

Maybe you should give up...
being reactive

———

D o you know what the worst type of pain is? I'll give you a clue. It's not your business failing, your relationship ending or never reaching your dreams. It's not breaking your leg, losing your biggest client or even watching your beloved pet die of old age. In fact, it's not any one big, terrible experience that overwhelms you with a flood of hurt in a particular moment. This type of pain is called acute pain. It hurts a lot all at once, but after a while, the pain goes away and you move on with your life.

No, the worst type of pain is the kind that doesn't actually hurt all that much...but never goes away. This is called *chronic pain*. Even though it disrupts you every day, it's not bad enough to push you to do something drastic to fix it. So you just put up with it, normalizing and using coping mechanisms to deal with it, until eventually it simply becomes part of who you are and something you've accepted as how your life has to be.

Like that bad lower back. Sure, you could probably improve it by not spending 12 hours in front of a computer. Or if you prioritize regularly stretching, exercising more or seeing a specialist. But all that sounds like a lot of hard work, especially when you're already busy. So instead, because you've had it for so long, you're just used to it, so the easier thing to do is just hobble along and take painkillers to numb the pain. Again, as bad as it is, it's not bad enough to make it a priority or to do something drastic to fix it.

And it's the same for putting up with problems in your relationship, feeling uncomfortable in your body, or accepting the stage you're at in your career. While you know things could and should be better, rather than doing anything drastic to change what is happening, you just complain about the situation as a painkiller to cope with how you feel.

Looking back to 2012 when I hit my lowest point, I realize now that when I was overweight, trapped in a job I hated and going through the motions, it wasn't that I didn't want to change. I knew I needed to. But at the same time, changing seemed like so much more work than *just coping*, especially since I had so many other things that also needed my attention. I had to go to work, keep on top of errands, look after my family and pay my bills, along with the never-ending list of responsibilities that come with being an adult. That's before finding time to exercise, make healthy meals or see friends. Honestly, just trying to keep up was exhausting, and most of my energy was spent simply trying to make it through the day.

Because of that, when it came to making changes in my life, I'd often find myself making all sorts of excuses about how it wasn't the right time, I was too busy or that I'll get to it eventually. I kept telling myself that even though I was unhappy, one day I'd turn it around and finally take control of my life. Honestly, I don't know if I truly believed it or not. Either way, it allowed me to keep a glimmer of hope that one day life would be better. The reality is though, all that did was further numb the pain. Because of that, I delayed my progress and happiness for nearly two years.

Sure, I had brief stints of motivation, but like New Year's resolutions, they would quickly get pushed to the bottom of the priority list. Today would turn into tomorrow, then next week, then next month. And in the blink of an eye, another year would be gone, and I'd still be no further along. That's why allowing life to happen to you and living in a state of chronic pain is the biggest reason we get stuck in a self-sabotaging cycle. Subconsciously, you see the ongoing pain of your situation as hurting less than the potential discomfort of changing it.

Yet all the time you hear about people who get a severe health diagnosis, go through a near-death experience, or reach a point of no return in their job, and what happens? Almost overnight they change their mentality and shift their actions and behaviors. Why? Because something happened that made the acute pain of change less painful than the chronic pain of the situation that they're in. All of a sudden, the thought of dying or getting severely sick hurts more than the struggle of eating healthy and exercising. The thought of reaching the end of their life unfulfilled hurts more than getting a new job or potentially failing in their business. The thought of living their life in an unhappy relationship hurts more than the idea of being alone.

Whatever they were accepting, suddenly became so painful that the reasons to change something became bigger than the excuses not to. This is why they were able to take massive action to turn their lives around without the mental resistance that weighed them down before.

The good news is that you don't *need* a near-death experience or something similarly drastic to be pushed to the point of making a change. Instead, you can make a decision right here and now that you are done with accepting how things are. That you're done with simply making it through the day. That you're done with being stuck. And that instead, you're going to do whatever it takes to take control of your life.

The best part is that you can do this any time you want! Because here's the reality: *doing this is entirely within your control*. At any point, you can make a decision to give up tolerating and accepting that this is how life has to be. Deciding instead that you are going to start consistently taking the actions you need to create the life you want. *Deciding* though, while it's sobering, it's not enough. Especially if you don't want to fall into the same old traps of short-lived motivation that leads to self-sabotage. That's why for this time to be different, you need to give up on the idea that your life is happening to you, and instead embrace the fact that you are in control of your life. In other words, you can either stay reactive or get proactive.

This is why the first barrier you need to break down is giving up on being controlled by the world around you. Knowing how to do that comes down to understanding the concepts of *cause and effect*.

Cause and effect

In life, you're either at cause, or you're at effect. No exceptions. And which side you fall into will directly determine everything from how you deal with challenges to your mental state, to the way you view the world and the actions you take every day. Most people are oblivious to how much cause and effect impacts their life. That's why once you understand and embody what I'm about to share with you, it can completely alter your perspective, helping you recognize that you have far more control over your life than you think.

I was originally introduced to the idea of cause and effect by one of my first mentors and it's an understatement to say it changed my life. Not just professionally, but also in a personal capacity, as it has transformed how I think, react and view the world. Since then, I've further built on this concept, developing and adding my own insights, findings and methods. It has become the foundation of the work I do with my clients. Whether I'm talking to a CEO running a billion-dollar business or a nine-to-five professional with an office job, this is the first thing I teach them.

Now, when I talk about being at effect, what I mean is allowing outside forces, whether it's other people, your environment, the past, or your problems, to dictate how you think, feel, react and behave. In this mindset, you let those factors determine your reaction rather than you controlling your response. In other words, you are *at the effect* of what is happening outside of yourself.

For instance, let's say you're working on a project and a member of your team makes a mistake and your reaction is to get frustrated and lose your temper. That's you being at the effect of them and what they did. Or you want to go to a fitness class or post a video on social media to promote your business, but you're scared of what other people will say or think, so you don't do it. That's you being at the effect of others and worried about their judgment. Or later you want to go for a run, but then it starts pouring with rain, so you stay in and tell yourself you'll do it another time. That's you being at the effect of the weather.

The problem with all of these situations is that you are not empowering yourself. Instead, you're allowing something that is outside of your control to dictate your actions, feelings and reactions. After all, there are so many solutions in every one of those scenarios. Take the running example; you could have gone to the gym, worked out at home, attended a class or even gone out in the rain. Yet because something got in the way of your original plan, rather than looking for other solutions, you allowed that external factor to influence the action you took.

Like I said, being at effect is anytime you allow something outside of you to dictate how you think, feel, react or behave. This is vital to understand, because *most people live their lives in a state of effect,* constantly reacting to what's going on around them. This state of mind negatively impacts everything you do, because when you are governed by your emotions and reactions, you block yourself from making the right decisions, taking the right actions or showing up as the best version of yourself. In other words, being at the effect of the world around you is a huge contributor to the chronic pain you feel in your life. Especially when you've been living this way for years, maybe even your whole life, which is why it's instinctive. It's automatic. It's familiar. It may even be comfortable—or at least more comfortable than trying *not* to do it!

Think about the last time you got really angry over something you couldn't control. Maybe someone cut you off in traffic, you had to stand in a long line when you were in a hurry, or a piece of technology wasn't working when you needed it to. You being angry had literally no impact on the situation— it didn't fix the tech, move the line faster or punish the other driver. All it did was make you frustrated, angry and impatient, not to mention, blind to any potential solutions. Any other time, you could see that those aren't good or helpful reactions. But in that moment, being angry was *the most important thing to you.* When you're at effect of things you can't control, you want to feel back in the driver's seat, and anger makes you feel like you're making a difference on your outcomes because you feel like you're doing something—even though you're not. Not only that, but often that reaction can make things worse. Not just for you, but for those around you. Like when you lose your temper at a member of your team who's late to a meeting or a waiter who made a mistake with your order. Sure, you feel powerful in the moment. But all you getting angry to make yourself feel better does is make the other person feel worse for their mistakes—and if they're at effect too, they'll probably want to react with just as much anger as you did.

That's why it is so important to recognize that there is a huge difference between a reaction and a response. While a response is thoughtful, a reaction is impulsive. Breaking that cycle is all about slowing down, processing the situation and understanding what is going on, so that you can then *choose* how you respond to it.

I found myself in this exact position a few months ago. I was sitting on a train and across from me was a group of kids who were shouting and screaming. I remember just sitting there on the edge of my seat, getting beyond frustrated that they wouldn't shut up. After a few minutes though, I realized I was completely at effect. The reality was that the kids weren't annoying me—instead, *I was choosing to get annoyed* by what they were doing. After all, there were so many solutions to my problem. I could put in headphones and turn up my music, focus on something outside the window, get back to my work or simply move seats. Yet because I was so fixated on the problem, I completely overlooked all the alternatives. It was only when I took a moment to slow down, understand why I felt the way that I did, and process what was going on, that I could change my response.

Getting this right isn't about making you immune to your emotions. You're only human, your emotions will always be there, and taking control of your response isn't about making you numb to what is going on around you. Instead, it's about getting you to focus on what you can control. Which, in every situation, is *your own response*. I know this can be tough to wrap your head around—especially if you've spent most of your life in the world of effect. Just the idea that you can change your response can be a difficult pill to swallow. That's because being at effect is both comfortable and chronically painful. We're used to it, it makes us feel powerful and in control even when we're not, and in the moment, it can feel really hard to do anything else.

But the good news is, you can give up being at effect. You can give up spending your days in a state of reaction. And you can give up allowing life to simply happen to you. And when you do, you'll start to see how much control you truly have.

External versus internal effect

Once you understand what I'm sharing with you, it'll become easy to see when you're at effect or reacting to something happening to you. Especially since you'll know what to look out for. On the train, when I was faced with those kids yelling and screaming, it only took a few short moments for me to realize I was being at effect. The more you practice this awareness, the easier it will become for you. What's not so easy, though, is realizing when you're being at the effect of *yourself*.

Going back to the introduction, remember how I spoke to you about how your brain causes an internal battle to keep everything the same? Where it puts negative thoughts, behaviors and habits in your way, that cause you to sabotage yourself? On a deeper level, this is your subconscious mind keeping you trapped in a state of effect. You are allowing something that happened in your past to influence your present, in turn sabotaging your future success.

The problem with this tendency is that it isn't as easy to notice as someone cutting you off in traffic. The reckless driver is external, as you can see it playing out in front of you. The voice in your head however is internal, making it far more subtle. Especially since at times you'll be so used to that way of thinking, that it's simply your default programming. It leaves you oblivious to the fact that those negative thoughts are keeping you at effect and stopping you from taking the actions you need to take.

The way you can tell this is happening is when the voice in your head tries to talk you out of what you need to do. Instead of putting yourself out there, you start to doubt yourself, fear you'll fail, worry you'll be judged or rejected. Whenever you start to justify how things are, procrastinate or make excuses to put off what you know you should be doing, you are at effect. This internal narrative is based on the experiences you've been through in your life. The environments, people, and events you've been exposed to have created beliefs about how life has to be. As a result, they become so deeply ingrained within you that they're just played out as stories in your head.

Let's say you tried to get involved with sports at school, but the other kids made fun of you because you weren't very good. Understandably, this made you feel insecure, and you started to believe that you just weren't good at physical activities. Fast forward 20 or 30 years and you want to get in better shape... but every time you think about going to the gym, your brain tells you that you suck at sports, you'll just embarrass yourself and everyone there will laugh at you. So you decide to not even try. See how this works? If you're settling for a job you hate, that may go back to when a teacher told you that you'll never amount to anything, and you developed the belief that you'd better take whatever you were given, because it's the best you could hope for. If you're afraid to ask out that person you see at the coffee shop, you may believe you're not good enough for them, because your toxic ex-partner called you ugly and useless, so you internalized the belief that you don't deserve love.

Notice how in these three examples your beliefs were molded by other people you interacted with or the environments you were in. You subconsciously interpreted the situation and made conclusions about what it meant, without stopping to question whether it was actually true. If anything, you didn't even recognize what you were telling yourself—instead, you immediately went to those thoughts and accepted them as your reality.

This is why it's so important to start questioning what these moments actually mean. Were you really bad at all sports? Were you really a failure? Were you really unworthy of love? Or is that just what you've been telling yourself?

One of my favorite stories that puts this into perspective is the story of the elephant and the peg. In this story, there's a baby elephant in a zoo, and at a young age the zookeepers tie it to a peg in the ground that's strong enough to stop it from breaking free and running away. As the elephant gets older and stronger, it could easily rip that peg out of the ground. But it never does, and the zookeepers never have to replace it with a bigger or stronger peg. Why? Because the elephant made a decision when it was younger that it couldn't break free, so it doesn't even try.

And it's the same for you. All of these beliefs that are keeping you pegged down are because something happened to you in your life that caused you to take on a thought pattern about how life *has to be*. And you've become so used to thinking that way, that you believe it's real, never stopping to question it. When in reality, they're nothing more than stories in your head. But here's the secret about these stories from your past: *they aren't true*. They're just your unconscious mind making a desperate attempt to get you to accept that this is the way that life has to be. That's why, if you can change your story, you can change your life. You can break the control they have over you. And you can set yourself free.

To make that happen though, you have to start pushing yourself to be at cause rather than at effect. That's how you're going to see for yourself that those negative thoughts are nothing more than stories. That's how you'll give up on all your beliefs about why you can't do something, so that you can get out of your way and push yourself to see who you can become. And as you prove to yourself what is actually possible, you'll be able to let go of what happened and come up with new stories about the life that you can live.

Never forget that your past doesn't have to define your future, unless you let it. Which is why you can make a decision that you're going to let go of what happened, stop holding yourself back and finally start living the life that you deserve.

Taking back control

Remember, you are never going to be in complete control of what's going on around you. What's the one thing you can always control though? How you choose to respond to it. In fact, this is so important I'm going to say it again and highlight it...

You are never going to be in complete control of what's going on around you, but the one thing you can always control is how you choose to respond to it.

In contrast to being at effect, this is what putting yourself at cause looks like. As in, you are making yourself the cause of your own responses to what happens to you. When you put yourself at cause, you can recognize that if you created a problem, then you have the power to fix it. Or even if you didn't create it, you can figure out a solution, determine your response, and/or control how you react.

While this may not be its true definition, if we take the word "responsible" and break it down, we get "response-able". As in, able to choose how you respond. In its simplest form, creating this shift from effect to cause comes down to you being responsible for your own actions, thoughts and reactions. When you do this, the problem and situation will be the same, but the way you look at them will be completely different. A simple but powerful example of changing that response came up recently in a client session. On the call, my client shared that earlier that week he was stuck in traffic, turning a 15-minute commute into well over an hour. In the past, he'd be fuming, honking his horn and shouting at other cars to move. Yet this time, he was completely unphased and calm. Upon reflection, he realized that his past frustrations were due to him being at the effect of the situation. But now, by slowing himself down and putting what was going on into perspective, he was able to consciously become aware of his reaction. Doing so allowed him to recognize that getting angry wouldn't change anything or improve what was happening. After all, he'd be stuck in traffic regardless of how frustrated he is, so there was no point getting stressed over a situation he couldn't change. By recognizing this, he was able to change his response, allowing him to let go of his frustration and calmly finish his commute.

The key thing to take away here is that his past reactions were due to him getting caught up in and reacting to the moment. Which was why he was only able to change his response by slowing down, processing what was happening and shifting his focus to what he could control. I know that this may sound simple, but like my client, once you embody what I'm sharing with you, then simply recognizing you are being at effect may be enough for you to change (or at least mitigate) your reaction.

Remember, being at effect is allowing something that is out of your control to impact the way you think, feel or react. So anytime you feel yourself getting stressed, angry, frustrated, overwhelmed or controlled by your emotions—you're probably at effect. And once you realize that, you can remind yourself that how you respond is a choice. From there, you can focus on what you need to do or how you can let it go. I'm not saying this is easy, but if you want to stop allowing life to happen *to you* and instead feel in control, then you have to be totally at cause for the majority of the time. If you aren't, your brain will keep you in a reactive state, where you'll focus on what is wrong, instead of what you can do about it.

Let's say you have a problem at work and you need to call a client to explain. You know it's going to be a difficult conversation you'd rather avoid, and you're tempted to just put it off. But the reality is that the problem isn't going to go away, which is why putting it off will only keep you trapped in a state of effect. Not only does this waste time and energy, it also leads to unnecessary stress and overwhelm, as well as risking the problem (and the client's reaction) becoming even worse if you delay—all of which could be avoided or reduced by just picking up the phone earlier. Now, making the call may not magically make the problem go away, but once you face the issue, you can figure out what you need to do next to fix the problem or move forward. The same applies to everything else in your life. From starting that project to hitting the gym, mustering the courage to speak to that person or working on your goals. If you want to make progress, then you have to push yourself to take action and face what you need to do.

A big part of developing this mindset is realizing that you and you alone are responsible for creating results in your life. This is why to create change and momentum, you need to put yourself at cause by reminding yourself that only you can make it happen. Every time you delay, procrastinate or avoid what you should be doing, you're falling back into a state of effect, where you focus on all the reasons why you can't, don't want to or don't feel like it, rather than turning to the reasons why you should or need to get it done.

Obviously, putting yourself at cause doesn't mean all your problems or triggers will magically go away. You will still have moments of anger and frustration, and times you procrastinate or want to put things off. In those moments, what matters is *how quickly you empower yourself to take back control.* That's why before taking any other kind of action, you have to give up on being at the effect of the world around you. Because until you do, your life, your reactions and ultimately your results will feel out of your control.

How to give up being at effect

If you're thinking that this sounds easier said than done, you're right, it is. Being at effect is a deep-seated habit for a lot of people, reinforced by both the comfort of familiarity and the ease of living with chronic pain over facing acute pain. Not only that, but a lot of the times you fall into being at effect through emotional reactions that happen almost instantly. You may not even realize what happened until hours or days later. Or you may know exactly what you're doing, but feel unable to stop or snap out of it.

What you will find though, is that as you develop this mind-set, you will have a far easier time letting go of setbacks. You will respond far better to challenges. And you will be bothered far less by issues that in the past, completely threw you off your game. Every time you break away from being at effect and take control of how you respond, it will become easier. With that being said, there are several practices that will make this mental shift easier to achieve.

Cultivate awareness

There's a huge difference between a reaction and a response. While a reaction is impulsive, a response is controlled. The first step towards being able to put yourself at cause and determine your response is to recognize when you are being at effect in the first place. In doing so you'll be able to develop your awareness and better understand how you think, feel, behave and react. In order to do this, throughout the day, practice noticing when you are at effect. Essentially, you're looking for any time you feel stressed, angry, sad, frustrated, overwhelmed or whatever the heightened negative emotions may be.

Then, whenever you find yourself in that state, force yourself to stop, take some deep breaths and imagine mentally taking a step back from what's happening. From there, ask yourself why are you at effect right now? What's causing you to feel this way?

What's key here is the deep breaths. When you go into that heightened state, your blood pressure and cortisol levels go up, which is why, at times, you feel cloudy or unable to focus. There's no way you can make the right decisions or act at your best in this state, which is why by stopping to breathe, you will lower those levels, allowing you to feel calmer and more grounded. It's one of the approaches ER nurses take to keep themselves in control during an emergency.

Forcing yourself to slow down will also allow you to detach yourself from the situation. Instead of getting caught up in what is happening, you can bring into your awareness the present and what is really going on. Doing so will help you understand why you're in a heightened or emotional state—maybe you're getting frustrated over a mistake that was made, feeling anxious over an upcoming meeting, procrastinating over a project you need to start or fearing attending a class. Whatever it is, take a moment to get clear on what's happening and why you're feeling at effect from it.

From there, remind yourself you have two choices. You can either stay at effect by allowing yourself to continue focusing on what went wrong, the problem at hand or what is happening, wasting time and energy you can never get back. Or, you can put yourself at cause by shifting your focus to the present and what you need to do about it.

Sometimes just recognizing you have a choice in how you handle the situation is exactly what you need to feel more in control. So instead of reacting, slow down and think about how you can empower yourself in that moment. What action do you need to take? What can you do about this? Doing this is going to go a long way in helping you create the internal shift needed to give up on being at the effect of the world around you. That's why I highly advise making this a priority, where instead of carrying how you feel into whatever you do next, you allow yourself to process and let go of what happened. For instance, after a stressful meeting, you could go to the restroom, close yourself in a cubicle and go through the breathing process to release tension before you move on to your next task.

It's important to note that breaking away from being at effect isn't going to make you immune to reactions or emotions. At the end of the day, you're only human and emotions are part of who you are. Instead, the focus here is about you turning your reactions around and changing your response as quickly as possible. Instead of allowing a difficult situation to ruin the rest of your day, you can change the way you feel. That's why becoming in tune with yourself and how you react is so essential. While most people are oblivious to these behaviors, you'll have the self-awareness to be able to recognize, understand and then change your response.

I do know that at times it isn't quite that simple. Despite your best efforts you still can't shake how you feel. Sometimes, consciously slowing down and processing what has happened is simply not enough. That's why I developed the next step.

The 15-minute rule

When you face a setback or difficult situation, instead of reacting, it helps to go through a mental process where you stop, observe what is happening, digest what is going on and only then choose how you respond to it. By forcing yourself to slow down, you'll be able to see and understand the situation for what it is, making it easier to break the cycle of your emotions taking over while you are reacting to what life throws at you.

The problem for a lot of people is that they try to bottle up and hold in how they feel. Because of that, they then carry that energy into everything else they do. Like when you have a bad day at work and you take the frustrations home with you, causing you to snap at your kids or partner. Or you get stuck in traffic and spend the rest of the day on edge, stressed and over-whelmed. The issue with holding in those emotions is they keep you trapped at effect. Only now because you're already in a heightened state, it makes it even more likely that the next chal-lenge, frustration or inconvenience will tip you over the edge. That's why if you want to feel in control, then you need to give up carrying those emotions with you by allowing yourself to process them so that you can let go and move on.

One of my favorite ways to do that is what I call "the 15-min-ute rule". Whenever you find yourself emotionally charged or your emotions are getting the better of you, give yourself 15 minutes to process and deal with them, working through how you feel, then commit to letting go of that emotional state, so you can move past it.

During that time you may want to go for a walk, meditate, listen to music, do a brief workout, or go through whatever you need internally to process and move on. At the end of the 15 minutes, commit to stopping, taking some deep breaths, and imagining that with every exhale you are releasing and letting go of whatever negative emotion you're feeling. When you feel calm and grounded, shift your focus to what you need to do to move forward. Whatever you do, set a timer, then when the 15 minutes are up, take a big, deep breath and commit to moving on.

What if there's no time? When you're busy, it can feel like there's no way that you can simply drop everything and go for a walk just because you are stressed. In those moments it's essential to remind yourself of the negative impact that holding onto these emotions will have on the rest of your day. Because even though it may not feel like the right time, is stepping away for 15 minutes that big a deal? Especially if it allows you to come back grounded, focused and in control?

Negative language traps

As you start to become more aware of times you are at effect, you'll also start to notice certain words you instinctively use in those situations—words that give you permission to be at effect rather than at cause, words that convince you that you're not really responsible for the situation at play and can't take control of it.

You'll probably find several words and phrases that are uniquely yours, but here are the five I see come up most often.

1. *"Makes me"*

"She makes me angry."
"What he's doing makes me so frustrated."
"The rain makes me sad."

"This meeting makes me anxious."

"Makes me" implies that someone or something can make you feel or behave a particular way. But remember, you have the ability to choose how you respond to any given situation. Even though it may not always feel like it, the way you feel and react is always completely under your control. It's like when your partner does something that makes you angry. The reality is they haven't made you angry, instead, you are choosing to get angry as a reaction to what they did.

It's vital to recognize that no one can *make you* do or feel anything. Once you become aware of that, you can control your mood, reactions and responses.

Solution: replace *"this makes me feel that way"* with *"I feel that way right now"*.

---

2. *"Hope"*

"I hope I can do this."
"I hope I can get to the gym later."
"I hope I get these results."

With *"hope"* you're essentially saying that you're hoping the stars are going to align, the planets are going to come together and everything is going to magically work out. This puts your results into the hands of external factors, implying that you have little to no influence on the outcome, meaning you're already at effect before you even start. It's like when someone goes on a diet saying *"I hope I can lose some weight"*. Instead of taking responsibility to eat healthier and exercise, they're essentially saying that getting results is out of their control. Before they even start, they've given themselves an excuse and justification for failing in the future.

Now, there are exceptions. If you've done everything you can for a job interview or pitch to a new client and now the outcome is out of your hands, you can say *"I hope I get it"*, because there's nothing more you can do to influence the outcome. *"Hope"* is only problematic if you're choosing to not take responsibility for an outcome or action within your control.

Solution: replace *"I hope..."* with *"I am going to..."*

---

3. *"Try"*

You're either going to do something, or you're not. There's no such thing as *"try"*. The problem with the word *"try"* is that it puts the problem on your future self. Like when someone asks you to go to an event, but you don't really want to go. Instead of saying no, you say *"I'll try and make it"*. What's happening in this moment is that you're essentially hoping that either your future self will get the motivation to go, or you'll think of an excuse not to. And if you don't go, you can then justify not making it because at least you said you'd *try*.

I used to do this all the time when I was first attempting to get in shape. Telling myself I'll try and go to the gym later. When really, deep down I was hoping something would come up, so I wouldn't have to go. It's no wonder it didn't work. I was *attempting* to get in shape, not actually doing it.

Saying *you'll try* is deceitful, because when you use it, you think you're putting yourself at cause, but really, you're staying at effect by giving yourself an out before you even start.

Solution: replace *"I'll try"* with *"I will"* or *"I won't"*.

---

4. *"If"*

"If I get this right."
"If I stick to this plan."
"If I can finish early on Thursday we'll go for dinner."

"If" is it implies that getting results is out of your control. Whether you want to lose weight, start a business, prioritize date night or anything else you need to get done, by using *"if"*, you keep yourself in a state of mind where you don't fully believe it will happen.

That in itself will keep you at effect, as not only will it cause you to view the outcome of the situation as down to chance, it will also prevent you from taking action because you already have an excuse.

Solution: replace *"if"* with *"when"*.

5. *"Should"*

We all have things in our life we feel like we *should* be doing.

"I should read more books."
"I should go to bed on time."
"I should get some exercise."

"Should" implies there's no feeling of urgency or necessity. Often with the things you *should* be doing, you'll end up in the world of effect, waiting for the right time or allowing something that seems more important in the moment to take priority. Whereas if you have something in your life that you *must* do, then regardless of what's going on, you find a way to do it. Which is why if you keep telling yourself you *should* be doing something, but you don't do it, then that raises the question—why not? Because if you don't actually want to do it, then make a decision to stop forcing yourself and let it go. Failing to follow through will only keep you in a world of effect where you beat yourself up for it, feel guilty or dwell on what you did or didn't do. These negative feelings and emotions could have been avoided by not putting yourself in situations you don't want to be in.

If however, it's something you truly want, then raise your standards and commit to following through.

Solution: either replace *"should"* with *"must"* or *"will"*, or decide to let go, and do something you *want* to do instead.

You can start to see from all of this how important language is, especially when it comes to how you speak to yourself. It's amazing how a simple shift in a word can completely alter your actions, focus, reactions and beliefs.

This is one of my favorite things to do with clients, as I find that about three weeks into the process, they catch themselves as soon as these words come out of their mouths, immediately saying *"I'm at effect"* before I can even point it out. As you practice watching out for your language choices, I bet you'll do the same!

One thing I can guarantee is that now that you know this, you'll constantly hear these phrases coming up in everyday conversations. Anytime someone is making excuses, justifying what went wrong, blaming someone for how they feel or saying how it can't be done, you'll hear these words. And because of it, you'll be able to see how they are at effect and why they're stuck and not getting results!

You won't get this right straight away, and that's okay. By regularly bringing these negative language traps into your awareness, you'll become far more aware of what you are focusing on and what you need to do to change your response. Over time, that will change your thought patterns and how you view the world.

Proactive reflection

When I'm working with my private clients, one exercise I get them to do is to take some time each day to reflect on what happened, the situations where they found themselves at cause and effect, and how they handled them. To do this yourself, at the end of each day, get a piece of paper and draw two columns.

You can also do this in a spreadsheet, on your phone, or any-where else that works for you. On one side, write down three situations that went right because you were at cause and three situations that went wrong because you were at effect, along with what was your responsibility in that situation and what you need to learn from it.

For instance, let's say you wasted an hour scrolling through the newsfeed rather than working on that report. Your responsi-bility was that you should have put down your phone and got to work. With that in mind, maybe you need to turn off your phone during work periods or remove certain apps that distract you.

On the positive side, maybe you needed to have a difficult conversation, so instead of putting it off, you faced it, got to the bottom of a problem and took the first step towards resolving it. This shows you how dealing with these issues sooner rather than avoiding them is helpful and needs to be your normal approach.

Gaining this clarity is a key part of growth. Especially since most people live their lives going through the motions, rarely stopping to think about what happened or what they can learn from it. Not only that, but they also tend to dwell on what they did wrong, often overlooking what went right or the progress they've made. That's why these reflections are your greatest opportunity to start building momentum and taking control. Because by taking responsibility for the good and bad in your life, you'll be able to start seeing the bigger picture of what is actually going on. This in turn will help you build your confi-dence and intuition, along with your ability to navigate future challenges. Think of it like an athlete watching their game foot-age and using it to figure out what they did, how they performed and how to improve for the future. This is how they gain their edge, and it's a vital practice used to help them become the best version of themselves. And it's the same for you.

Remember though, this is never about blame. You're not dwelling on the past, beating yourself up over mistakes or allowing yourself to be at effect over what you can't change. Instead, you are learning for the future. Always remember that every mistake is only a bad thing if you keep repeating it. Whereas if you learn what to do next time and you follow through with it, then that mistake was actually a good thing, as it enabled you to do better. Like I said before, this is all about how you choose to look at what is happening, which in itself is you choosing to be at cause regardless of what is going on around you.

To follow through with this exercise, commit to setting aside some time each day for at least the next two weeks where you create your table and reflect on what happened. This shouldn't take more than a few minutes, but the insights you gain from this will be invaluable. Also, take some time each week to go back through your reflections so that you can get a more macro picture of what happened. You can also keep the exercise sheets almost like a journal for you to look back on later to see how far you've come.

Why being reactive is the first thing to give up on

Now you have some ideas about how to give up on letting the world control you, you may be wondering why start here. Why is this the biggest boulder?

The reason why we're focusing on this first is that every other aspect of this book is related to it. Because of that, this mindset is going to be the foundation of everything you do— not just in this book, but in every area of your life going forward. In fact, there's a good chance that the reason why you've struggled to get results in the past has been due to you being at effect. That's why in order to give up on everything else that is getting in your way, you will need to put yourself at cause, focus on what you need to do and take action on it.

It's an understatement to say that mastering this way of thinking is essential to your success on this journey. Especially since most of the problems in your life right now could probably be solved by putting yourself at cause and facing what you need to face. But the more you get stuck in effect, the more your focus will go to all the reasons not to do something. Which in turn will stop you from moving forward.

Regardless of what's going on though, it's important to remember that you and you alone are responsible for creating results in your life. That's why if you want to create change and build momentum, you have to stop living in a world of effect where life is happening to you, and instead, you need to focus on what you can control.

The best part is you can mentally go through this process anytime you find yourself getting in your own way. When you're procrastinating, overwhelmed, angry or avoiding what you need to do, put yourself at cause by reminding yourself that only you can control how you respond. From there, focus on what you need to do and then push yourself to act on it.

It's that simple. Definitely not always easy. But it is that simple. And once you get this right, you'll transform the results you are able to create in every area of your life.

Once you adopt this mindset, the entire game will change for you. Not only will you gain a new level of confidence, you'll also create a newfound belief that regardless of the challenge in front of you, that you can handle it and get through. Instead of falling victim to your situations, circumstances and environments, you'll be able to show up as the best version of yourself in everything you do.

CHAPTER 2

Maybe you should give up...
letting fear control you

———— ≡ ————

R eactivity is the first boulder to drop because it prevents you
from thinking you can take action in the first place. After
all, when you're at effect or out of control, taking action
or making a change feels like it's not even possible. So once
you've given up on being reactive, and you've recognized that
you and you alone are responsible for creating results in your
life, you'll be empowered to take the action you didn't think
you were capable of before. Great! You're all set now, right?

Well, not exactly. Now you have a new problem: taking
action is scary. In fact, after reactivity, the biggest thing that
stops people from living the lives they want is fear. You know
you can take action, make changes and improve your life. You
know you have the capability and control to do those things. You
likely even feel empowered and motivated to do those things.

But you still don't do them...because It's scary to step
away from the status quo. This is the other side of chronic pain.
When you're at effect, chronic pain becomes easier to deal with

because *you don't think you can fix it* (and so you never try). When you're afraid, on the other hand, chronic pain becomes easier to deal with because *the alternative (the acute pain of making a change) is too scary to face.*

Fear reinforces all of the mental barriers in your head, creating stories that cause you to procrastinate, overthink and doubt yourself, which in turn stop you from doing the things you know you should be doing to live or create the life you want. It can be so frustrating, especially when despite knowing what you need to do, you just can't bring yourself to face what's standing in your way. After years of feeling and behaving this way, those stories in your head feel real. They become so ingrained inside you, that they just become how you view the world, so even the idea of standing up to them feels paralyzing.

It's like a bungee jumper standing on top of a cliff. The longer they stand there, the harder it becomes to jump, as the fear continues to build up inside them until they feel paralyzed. That problem could be immediately solved by just jumping, but because they've delayed and got stuck in their own head, the fear has taken over and they can't move. And it's the same for you with many of your goals, problems and challenges in your life, where you too could solve them by pushing yourself to take action. Sure, it may not fix everything or make the problem go away, but it would take you one step further along or remove the mental anguish that comes with avoiding what you know you need to do. Especially when you have to face it eventually anyway.

Not only that, but putting the action you want to take on hold often takes more energy than just getting it over with. We've all been there, where you sit around procrastinating over what you know you need to do, sometimes for hours. It's exhausting and by the end of the day it leaves you feeling worse than if you'd spent the day digging ditches...yet once you take action, you usually realize it wasn't all that bad!

So once you've given up on being at effect, the next boulder to give up on is fear. Once you know you can take action, and you've faced your fear of taking action, there's nothing to stop you from actually doing it.

What you're actually afraid of

The first step in giving up on letting fear control you is recognizing what you're actually afraid of. So let's start by looking at the three biggest fears that may be holding you back.

Failure

Let's be honest—failure is probably the biggest and most obvious thing most of us are afraid of. Putting yourself out there doesn't guarantee success. Giving something your all might still come up short. These possibilities are scary enough to keep many of us from taking any action for years.

A past client of mine, Susan, is a prime example of that. For years she had dreamt about breaking out of the corporate world and starting her own marketing consulting business. She had a long track record of delivering for the companies she'd worked for and she was fantastic at what she did. Despite that though, before we met, she had been delaying launching the business for several years, as she always felt like she was too busy or claimed it wasn't the right time. When we dived in deeper though, it turned out that these were just excuses she was telling herself to avoid taking action. In reality, she hadn't launched her consulting business because she was afraid that she wouldn't be good enough and it would fail, leaving her broke, jobless and back at square one.

If you find yourself thinking that things will never work, that you're not good enough, that you're not ready or questioning what if it all goes wrong, you're probably afraid of failure.

Success

People talk about the fear of failure all the time, but what is often overlooked is the fear of success. This fear can be just as self-sabotaging. It usually looks like this: just as you're on the verge of something great, you become overwhelmed with thoughts about how it'll all fall apart. As a result, you start to worry that you're not good enough, or you won't be able to handle the challenges ahead. You might even fear that your success will transform your life in a negative way, so you tell yourself you don't want it, after all. From there, a self-destructive cycle kicks in. You procrastinate, overthink, avoid what you know you need to do, or take an action that tears down all of the progress you've made. Like when after years of hard work, you get an interview for your dream job or a huge business opportunity. Instead of feeling excited, you start to convince yourself of all the reasons why it's not the right fit. Or after finally getting into a healthy relationship, you start to actively find faults in that person and push them away. The truth is, success can be terrifying, which is why your brain often programs you to shy away from it, doing everything it can to get you to stay in your current reality. Even if it means sabotaging all your efforts or coming at the expense of what you truly want.

I still remember the first sales call I ever had with a potential client. Going into the call I was so excited, as after years of studying, researching and building my skills, someone finally wanted to potentially work with me. As the call went on though, I started to panic, because for the first time, I was facing the reality that if this person said yes, I'd actually have to deliver. I could feel all that nervous energy build up inside me, as my self-doubt kicked in and I started to question whether or not I could actually do this. I think the person could sense this fear, which translated into uncertainty, as in the end, they didn't hire me.

If you're concerned that getting to the next level might turn you into someone you don't want to be, worried about how much work or time it will take, afraid that your positive outcome will draw negative attention or criticism, feeling like you're making promises you can't deliver on or wondering whether you actually want what you're working towards, you're dealing with a fear of success.

Rejection and judgment

While failure and success are fears about you, rejection and judgment are fears about other people. What will they say if you post a video, try to start exercising, start a business or ask them out for coffee? Will they laugh at you? Will they insult you? Worst of all, will they completely ignore and exclude you?

I'll never forget the first time I went to work out on my own in the gym. Walking into the weights area I was terrified by all these huge guys grunting in the corner staring at their biceps. I remember feeling so inadequate and out of place, and even though I may not have wanted to admit it to myself back then, I know now my biggest fear was that everyone there would laugh and judge me for being a beginner who had no clue what he was doing.

It's easy to take rejection and judgment to heart, where you view them as a sign of who you are as a person, that you are wrong or unworthy. Because if there wasn't something wrong with you, then you'd never have been rejected or criticized, right? The reality is that you often perceive these setbacks in a way that makes them out to be a far bigger deal than they actually are. As a result, it makes you feel far worse about them than you otherwise would. After all, even though they may hurt in the moment, in most cases, that pain is nothing more than temporary and something that you'll probably have forgotten about by next week.

If you aren't taking action because you're worried you'll get fired, laughed at, mocked, excluded, shut down, judged, criticized, trolled, hated or simply told *no*, then you've got some fear of rejection and/or judgment to deal with.

Why those things scare you so much

Failure, success, rejection and judgment are paralyzing. Why is it so hard to take action in the face of these fears? One thing all these fears have in common is that they're focused on how badly you believe a future event will turn out—and how you won't be able to handle that negative event when it happens. Whether it's chatting to an attractive person, delivering a presentation, going for a new job, starting a business or attending a fitness class, the story you're telling yourself is focused on how bad it's going to go, how you'll mess it up or why you won't be able to do it. It's frighteningly easy to fixate on those negative predictions and believe that story in your head is real.

Not only can this stop you from taking action toward what you want, it can also convince you that you don't want it after all! In your mind, the pain you are certain to face when it goes wrong is far worse than the potential relief or gain you get if it goes right. Remember, the fear of acute pain is scarier than the frustration of chronic pain!

Take my client Stephen, for example. A few weeks before we met he did a presentation which was met with some ruthlessly tough questioning by the team in the room. It put him on the spot, and because he didn't know the answers, it caused him to freeze and lose his train of thought, making the presentation a complete disaster. Everyone's probably had a presentation like that, where they were off their game, mumbled their words or forgot what they wanted to say. But despite dozens of previous pitches that went well, Stephen just couldn't shake this one off and move forward. Doing presentations is a huge part of his role as a founder in his business. He literally did them almost every day while they were fundraising and securing investment. Instead of looking at this disaster as an isolated incident, Stephen saw it as a sign that he was terrible at his job and therefore kept thinking he'll have disastrous presentations, which would directly cause the failure of the business. This fear brought up massive anxiety about all his upcoming meetings. It got so bad that the thought of giving another presentation had an almost paralyzing effect—even when talking about them with me he'd freeze and stumble on his words. He had lost all confidence in what he was doing. To make matters worse, shutting down like that just further reinforced his belief that he couldn't do presentations.

Another client, Jamie, faced a similar paralysis around attending networking events to find new business leads. Normally he loved going to them—he was a major people person, loved building relationships, and networking was the main way he grew his business. But now, just the thought of attending these events spiked his anxiety to the point he couldn't bring himself to leave the house. Understandably, this left him feeling trapped, as he just couldn't bring himself to take the main action that brought clients into his business. Turns out that what triggered this mindset shift had nothing to do with Jamie's ability to work a room. Instead, it had been a really tough year business-wise for him. He'd lost several clients and had to let a few team members go, and his once-thriving business was facing a long road to recovery. Jamie had convinced himself that everyone in the room at any networking event would judge him for those struggles, think he was a fraud and talk behind his back about how he was a failure. This belief made him so nervous that he'd break out in a sweat before he even walked into an event, which amplified his fear that people would stare, wondering what was wrong with him, and that upon walking into that room of judgment, he'd crumble and fall apart.

So even though he knew what he needed to do, this mental barrier had him frozen in place, and he just couldn't bring himself to face these events…which made his business struggle even more, as his cycle of self-sabotage meant that he wasn't filling his client pipeline through networking anymore.

Reframing fear

While being at effect creates stories in your head based on a previous experience, fear works exactly the same way. Except this time, the stories are about the future, not the past. By getting you to focus on how you may fail, won't be able to handle success, or how you'll be rejected, that's how your brain can keep you where you are. This is why it's so important to realize that *the story in your head isn't set in stone*. Each story that tells you how terrible things are going to be is just an assumption. It might as well be a guess. Sure, it *could* happen, but that doesn't mean it *will* happen. And even if it does happen, it probably won't be as awful as your brain says it will be. It might even be a positive experience!

Take failure, for instance. When you don't get the result you want, it's easy to relive that failure in your mind and convince yourself that it will keep happening. But will it really? Is that guaranteed? Just because something bad happened once, doesn't mean it'll happen again. And if anything, that negative experience is an opportunity to learn what *not* to do next time, so you *don't* fail again—or at least don't fail the same way twice. This is why every failure is a stepping stone towards finally getting it right.

Stephen had fallen into this exact trap when it came to his presentations. His fear of failure completely blinded him to the fact that *he'd already given hundreds of them*. And most of them had gone well—maybe they hadn't all been wildly successful, but he clearly knew how to do his job! That one disastrous presentation had literally been him having an off day. Yet he was so focused on the one time things went wrong, that he was completely overlooking all the times they went right. Not only that, but after that disaster, he knew exactly what he needed to do to get even better: prepare mentally ahead of time to handle tough questions, so he could be confident in dealing with similar situations in the future. Even though that one failure was painful, it was actually a positive, as it put him through an experience that forced him to grow and improve.

When Stephen was able to make these two mindset shifts, his fear evaporated. By doing so he was able to remind himself of his past successes, as well as better prepare himself for future challenges. This allowed him to visualize how he wanted to show up, playing out in his mind exactly how he wanted to conduct himself, speak with confidence and handle difficult questions. Unsurprisingly (at least to me), he knocked the next presentation out of the park.

The key here was the mindset shift. So let's look at how to reframe each of the three big fears.

Reframing fear of failure

As we just saw, breaking through a fear of failure is less about preventing a potential failure and more about realizing that any potential failure won't be as awful as you think.

Don't forget, that nagging voice in your head wants to convince you that failing is this terrible catastrophe, when in reality it's just part of the process of learning or doing something new. In fact, if you take any successful person and break down the ingredients of their success, you'll clearly see that failure plays a key role in what got them to where they are.

Just take Walt Disney. If you look at his backstory, you'll see he was once fired from a newspaper because he *lacked creativity*. A setback that started him on his own path, where eventually he went on to create one of the biggest and most creative companies of all time.

Obviously, it is scary when you focus all your energy on how badly something is going to go. But when you shift your focus to what you can learn from it, you get a whole new outlook on what is happening. The reality is that it is during failures and setbacks that you figure out what not to do, how to improve in the future or what you actually want. Not only that, but it's often in your biggest failures that you discover who you truly are, opening up new opportunities that you otherwise would never have found or even considered.

When you view failure and setbacks as simply stepping stones preparing you to succeed, you can take those experiences and use them to learn and grow. You can figure out how to improve for the future and ensure you don't fall into the same setbacks again. That's why failure is only truly bad when you make the same mistakes over and over again without learning from them.

Reframing fear of success

Fear of success is just fear of failure on a larger scale. Because when you can't handle success, or the things that go along with it, what happens? You fail. But looking at success as a potential failure to learn from won't work to counter the fear of success itself. Instead, reframing fear of success is about focusing on two things: capability and adaptability.

Capability means that you know how to achieve the success you want. And adaptability means that you'll be able to handle whatever happens in the process of achieving it—whether that's failure along the way or bigger challenges that show up afterward.

Let's say you're worried that if you get the promotion, you won't be able to deliver at the higher level of the new position. This is a completely understandable fear, especially when the stakes are higher and people are counting on you. Instead of allowing it to deter your new path, you can use that fear as a flashlight to shine a light on the areas you'll need to get better at to be successful in the position. For instance, maybe there's a new skill set you need to develop, which may require putting aside some time to read some books or take a course to help you be more prepared. Or maybe you need to get a coach or mentor to help you better understand the new responsibilities of the position and figure out how to approach it successfully. Or maybe it will help to sit down and re-examine your track record to remind yourself that you *are* ready for a step up!

It's also helpful to remember that even for the parts of your life where you do feel confident in your abilities, you didn't feel that way to begin with. Instead, you allowed yourself to try, to fail, to learn and grow. You didn't get it right the first time, and that was okay. Don't be afraid to cut yourself some slack, where rather than putting pressure on yourself to get the new position perfect from day one, you allow yourself to take the time needed to build your skills. By removing that weight from yourself, you'll be able to see your capability and adaptability as skills you can build over time, rather than inborn traits.

Reframing fear of rejection and judgment

I'm going to cut right to the chase on this one. The way to reframe fear of rejection and judgment is to remember two things:

1. Rejection isn't personal.
2. Judgment isn't about you.

Now, I know your brain is screaming at you right now that there's no way those two statements could be true. Rejection is personal, and judgment is about you, right? After all, you're the one being rejected and judged! Not so fast.

I remember several years ago before I became a coach, I interviewed for what seemed like my absolute dream job. And the interview went amazing—I brought my absolute A-game, answered every question confidently, and even hit it off with the interviewer as we went down a rabbit hole talking about gym routines and how working out was a huge part of the company culture. I knew I was a great fit and I was absolutely sure I'd get the job. But I didn't. I was completely crushed. I spent several hours after receiving the *"we went with a different candidate"* email, spiraling down into self-doubt, self-pity and self-loathing. I just knew I'd done something or said something wrong that caused the company to reject me. Eventually, I managed to pull myself together enough to reach out to the recruiter and ask if they had any feedback for me. It turned out that the company did think I'd be a great fit and would have loved to hire me. But there was one key aspect of the role I'd never done before, whereas the other candidate had experience doing it for years. This meant that despite the rapport we built, given the skills needed by the business, they had to go with the other candidate instead. Not getting the job still hurt! But it wasn't a personal rejection or a reflection on me as a person. In fact, it wasn't about me at all. And in the grand scheme of things, there was nothing I could have done differently to change the outcome.

When you get rejected, remember that you only know one side of the story—and that story is your perception of what happened and what you tell yourself it means. Chances are that what's really happening has nothing to do with you as a person, but everything to do with reasons or circumstances you may not even be aware of. It's almost never personal.

This brings me to the second statement to remember: judgment isn't about you. It's about the person making the judgment. When I first started my business, I used to struggle constantly when people left negative comments on my social media posts. Despite being new to creating content, I was trying my best, and I just couldn't understand how people could be so cold and cruel. Especially when their comments attacked me personally—my accent, how I look, the topics I teach, how and why I want to help people, etc. I would be depressed for days whenever people would come out of the woodwork to tear me and what I was doing apart. What I ultimately realized was that when someone tears you down, it's a reflection of their own pain and inadequacy. They're not doing it because you're wrong or bad, they're doing it because they feel bad about themselves, and the only way they know how to feel better is to try to make someone else feel worse than they do. Making you small is the only way they can feel big. So the next time you find yourself in this situation or facing this fear, remind yourself that no one who is successful spends their days trolling or tearing other people down. Instead, they're focused on furthering their own goals and ambitions, not wasting time belittling others, making snarky remarks or arguing with people on the internet. And this is key, because when you start to combat that judgment with empathy, wondering what has happened in that person's life to cause them to lash out, it can give you a whole new perspective on why it is happening. Does that make what they are doing right or justifiable? Of course not, but it does make it easier to deal with and let go.

Think back to how other people don't want you to put down the big rocks you're carrying around and start making changes in your life. Chances are the people giving you the most judgment are the ones doing the least with their own lives—they're feeling threatened and jealous by you taking action, so they're trying to get you to stop so they can feel better about not taking any positive steps themselves. Even if someone does judge you, the bigger question is whether you really want their opinion to stop you from living your life. One of my favorite quotes is *"if video games taught me anything, it's that when you encounter enemies, you are moving in the right direction"*. When you have huge goals and aspirations, whether it's in the workplace, online, in your business or any other area of your life, you will face adversity and criticism. But if you believe in what you are doing and are being true to who you are, then you have a duty to yourself to not be deterred by the thoughts of others.

Breaking through fear

Now you have some ways to reframe your fears of failure, success, rejection or judgment, to make them less paralyzing and easier to face. But even knowing how to reframe fears doesn't magically make the anxious thoughts go away. After all, when you're in a challenging or uncomfortable position, your emotions can quickly take over and cause you to react. When that happens, you can't think clearly or make sense of what is going on. And that makes reframing fear more diffi- cult. To break through fear, you'll need to interrupt your current patterns and behaviors. You need to learn to break the cycle of getting stuck in your own head and get a new perspective on the situation you're in. Here's what you're going to do next time fear is threatening your success.

First, stop what you're doing. Really stop whatever you are currently involved in, as you need to interrupt the pattern of the emotions you're feeling, so that you can mentally step back from it. Next, take a few big, deep breaths. This will lower your blood pressure, allowing you to calm down and making it easier to think clearly.

Once you're feeling calmer and more grounded, ask yourself these questions:

1. What am I anxious, uneasy or fearful about?
2. What specifically is causing me to feel this fear and anxiety?
3. What am I afraid will go wrong here? What's the worst-case scenario I'm worried about?
4. What if the opposite happened? What would happen if things went amazingly right?
5. Knowing the best and worst-case scenarios, what is *most* likely to happen?
6. Even if things do go wrong, is it really as big of a catastrophe as the story in my head tells me it is?

These questions are so impactful because they allow you to stop and break down the situation to see what is going on rather than spiraling into fear. This will help you see the situation for what it is, which in turn will make it far easier to face your fears and follow through with what you need to do.

Remember Jamie? The client who had developed a paralyzing fear of going to networking events and being judged? By going through these questions, he was able to realize that his fear was based on a situation that didn't actually exist. The reality was that no one in that room knew his business or what was going on behind closed doors. Meaning there was no possible way that they were judging Jamie for his business struggles. The story he was telling himself could not be true. Upon realizing that, he committed to facing his fear and later that week he attended a networking event. Now, just to be clear, this fear didn't suddenly go away. He still felt anxious. He still felt overwhelmed. He still really wanted to stay home. However, he had found a coping mechanism that enabled him to take action in order to get back on track.

Upon arriving at the event, Jamie first went to the restroom, locked himself in a stall, closed his eyes and breathed to calm himself down. He then put the situation into perspective by going through the questions I shared with you above. He was able to remind himself that the worst-case scenario of people judging him couldn't possibly be true, as no one knew his situation. He was also able to see that the best case would be meeting the right connections and landing some business. And based on the countless number of events he'd attended in the past, he knew that the most likely outcome would be that he'll meet some new people, have some good conversations and get to know more about what was going on with local companies.

After this practice, this situation no longer felt so bad. Rather than putting this huge pressure on himself, Jamie could just go in and do what he did best—connect with people and have fun doing it. By shifting his perspective, he was able to stop viewing this event as some huge, daunting endeavor and instead see it as something he will actually enjoy. The result? He had an incredible time, made some amazing new connections and gave such a good impression that they invited him back the following week to do a talk. This scenario was far away from the story he'd been telling himself about how this would turn out. In fact, it went so well that a year later he started running his own networking events!

Breaking through these fears all came from Jamie stopping, putting what was going on into perspective and shifting his focus from the past to the actions he needed to take in the future.

The truth about fear

The thing to remember about fear is that it's nothing more than a story. If you want to take back control, then you have to start questioning every story and challenge every fear. That means whenever you find yourself feeling anxious, focusing on how something will go wrong, or making assumptions about how a situation will play out, stop and question if you know this for certain, or if it's just a story you're telling yourself. If it's just a story, how else could it turn out? What action do you need to take?

With that in mind, my challenge to you is to think of one thing you've wanted to do but avoided out of fear, then face it.

That may mean attending that class, posting that video, applying for that job, asking that person out or facing that difficult conversation. Whatever it is, my challenge to you is to push yourself to act on it immediately (or schedule it to be done as soon as you can). By pulling off that band-aid you'll be able to take a huge weight off yourself—and even if you don't get the outcome you hoped for, you can move forward with your life knowing you faced your fear.

Now, I know the thought alone may be terrifying. What you need to realize though is that you are never going to know the alternative of any decision you make. Which is why you've got to decide—would you rather take your shot and possibly move forward, or not take it and stay where you are? Because at the end of the day, you'll never know what could happen or how a situation will play out unless you go through with it. And I know that it's scary, but the longer you delay, the more you'll build it up in your head, focusing on what *could* go wrong or all the reasons not to do it. Just like the bungee jumper standing on top of the cliff though, you too can immediately solve your problem by just *jumping into action.*

Whatever fear is currently holding you back, you can break the hold it has over you right now by taking action. By taking that step, chances are you'll see it was nowhere near as terrifying as the voice in your head made it out to be. Which in turn, will make it far easier for you to take action again in the future.

Instead of fearing failure, success, rejection or judgment, I encourage you to fear never having tried. Because at the end of the day, facing fear is part of the journey and it's a sign that you're pushing yourself to grow. And when you finally get to where you want to be, knowing all the fears you overcame along the way will make that victory even sweeter.

Part 2:

THE ROCKS

Reactiveness and fear had to be the first two states of mind to give up on—partially because they're the two biggest and heaviest rocks in your backpack. Feeling like your life isn't in your control and feeling too afraid to do anything are the most paralyzing states you can be in. More importantly, reactiveness and fear are the big nonstarters on this list. Being at effect makes it too easy to avoid taking action and just stay where you are. Fear makes it impossible to take action because just getting started is too scary.

That's why it's imperative to give up on those two mindsets first *so that you can get started taking the action you want to take.* We had to put down those boulders because they were literally too heavy to carry.

The next three rocks in your backpack aren't quite as big. They're not heavy enough to keep you from getting started. But they are still pretty heavy—heavy enough to tire you out and hold you back as you're starting to make progress. Worse, they make it easy for you to sabotage your own best efforts.

Think about it. You've retaken control of your life, faced your fear and got started on taking action...you're working hard, making progress, building momentum, and feeling positive about how things are going...and then, without warning, you shoot yourself in the foot and end up right back where you started.

It's beyond frustrating. What's the point of doing all this work and taking all this action in the first place if you're just going to torpedo it as soon as you start making progress?

That's why in the next chapter, we're going to learn how to give up on the three biggest ways we sabotage ourselves *during* our journeys toward better lives. These rocks are thinking short-term, fixating on the future and comparing yourself to other people.

CHAPTER 3

Maybe you should give up...
short-term thinking

"One extra cookie won't hurt. I want to treat myself."

"I worked hard today, I deserve a break. I'll get back to the gym tomorrow."

"I don't want to make that call now, I'll do it later."

"I know I can't afford it, but that's what credit cards are for."

"You only live once!"

Have you ever said any of those things to yourself? Statements like these may seem harmless, but they're not. They actually do immense damage to our progress and undo much of our hard work. Firstly, because they focus on feeling good in the short-term without considering the impact in the

53

long-term. And secondly, because they're easy to repeat without thinking.

Why you sabotage your long-term success

Suppose Peter wants a bar of chocolate every night, as it makes him feel good when he's had a long day. When Peter eats the chocolate, he's momentarily satisfied and feels good. Now, if this was the full story, then it would be a good one, as Peter has had his chocolate and he's happy.

But what if Peter is trying to lose weight and be more conscious of his health? Deciding to eat a chocolate bar at the end of a hard day may feel good at the time, but what about when he steps on the scale the next morning? What about when he checks in at the end of the week and his pants are still too tight?

Small actions like this may seem insignificant, but if you keep making them, they will compound like a snowball rolling down a hill. Regularly skipping your workout can lead to big health problems. Never speaking up in an important meeting could lead to issues in your company or not getting recognized for that upcoming promotion. Weeks or months of working late instead of making it home for dinner could lead to your relationship falling apart.

Let's say Peter continues his daily decision to eat a chocolate bar—sometimes because he's had a good day and wants to treat himself, sometimes because he's had a bad day and wants to comfort himself, sometimes because he's bored or tired, or just in the habit of doing it. He continues to gain weight, or at least gain *back* any weight he loses. Over time, his weight-loss efforts stagnate. His energy drops. His self-image suffers. He stops believing in himself, causing him to hold back and settle in his life. As a result, he doesn't get the success, fulfillment or happiness he desires, and ultimately, he doesn't live as long and dies feeling disappointed and regretful.

Okay, that may be a bit extreme, but it illustrates the point: *the small decisions you make today can and will impact your future for years to come.* And most of the small decisions we make today are designed to make us feel good in the short-term—often at the expense of success in the long-term. Now, don't get me wrong, I'm all for balance and enjoying life. If Peter decides that the occasional chocolate bar has a place in his new healthy lifestyle, that's okay. But one of the biggest lessons I've learned on my own journey is that if you truly want to reach your goals, then you have to recognize when your short-term thinking is coming at the expense of your long-term success. Because until you give up making decisions or basing your actions on this instant gratification frame of mind, it will keep holding you back.

There are two reasons we tend to choose short-term grati-fication over long-term success. Put simply, whatever we want to do in the short-term either feels good, or it *doesn't* feel bad. And because we want to feel good or not feel bad in the present moment, we don't stop to think about what impact that decision will have on our future. Or we justify it by saying how much we need that good feeling (or lack of bad feeling) right now.

This is especially true because in order to improve our lives in the long-term, we often have to make choices in the short-term that feel like a sacrifice, self-deprivation or uncomfortable self-discipline. Our brains are wired to avoid pain and discom-fort at all costs, so it's tough to prioritize *what you want most in your life* over *what you want right now.*

Like when someone offers you a doughnut when you just started a new diet. At the time, you desperately want it, and sure, it'll taste great, but those few minutes of pleasure could destroy your weight loss efforts. Especially if it happens every day. Or let's say you need to get started on an important project at work, but the project is complex and tedious and you really don't want to do it. So instead, you procrastinate, wasting hours scrolling through social media. Doing this once could put you behind by a few hours and make you have to work overtime to catch up. Doing it regularly for weeks will likely get you fired.

Because we focus on what we want in the moment, we view our actions in isolation, rarely stopping to think of the longer-term implications and how they affect our lives. This is made even worse by the fact that these initial actions are usually focused on pleasure, comfort or momentary satisfaction. So even though long-term they may be hurting us, mentally we view them as a positive—which is why passing on them often feels like a sacrifice, discomfort or pain. That's why if you want to take back control, then it is this instant gratification, focus on rapid rewards that you need to give up on.

How to give up on short-term thinking

It's tough to prioritize what you want most over what you want right now. Especially when it requires saying no, facing something you don't want to do, or feeling like you are depriving yourself of something you like. Yet it's in that tougher decision that you'll find the real growth you want.

That's why giving up on short-term thinking requires a mindset shift. Instead of focusing on how good it will feel right now to eat the piece of cake, put off the client call or go back to sleep when your alarm goes off 30 minutes earlier than usual, shift your focus to what you will gain in the future by making the harder or less pleasant decision in the present. Let's say your task for the day is to call your current list of prospects and set up sales presentations. Just by looking at that initial action, it's clear to see why you might not want to do that. Cold calling is uncomfortable at best and can be downright terrifying sometimes. So it would be really easy to decide not to do it today and put it off until you're feeling more confident or in the right mood (whenever that might be).

But when you shift to looking at what you might gain from picking up the phone now rather than putting it off, your perspective on the decision changes. You could start gaining some traction and building your confidence so you can grow your business or do your job really well. You could build on your relationships with people in your pipeline—even if they say no now, they might say yes later because they feel they got to know you better. You could close some clients and earn more money or put yourself on track for a promotion. You could start to get the recognition and success you desire. You could build a freer and richer life where you can provide for your family comfortably.

As you can see, some of these benefits are immediate and some build over time, but all of them stem back from changing your mindset around making the tougher decision in the present moment. And as you think about those potential gains, suddenly picking up that phone and getting started now seems more like a priority. Now you can see what you have to gain in the future, and how that is more important than avoiding discomfort now.

This is exactly how successful people make decisions. If you pick anyone you admire, you'll see patterns in how they approach decision-making in a similar way. Rather than focusing on the short-term pain or sacrifice involved in making and acting on a decision, they look at all the potential future benefits that decision could bring them. By looking at the bigger picture, they can think five steps ahead. In turn, they use that foresight, along with their goals and vision, to guide their actions. This also enables them to view the situation at a higher, more strategic level. Even when an initial action could lead to short-term losses or an outcome that, in isolation, could be seen as a failure, they can still move forward in good conscience, as they know it is merely a stepping stone towards the end goal. This is also why most successful people ignore criticism from people who aren't involved in their decisions or who don't know the reasons behind them—most of the time, the critics themselves are only seeing the short-term problems, not the long-term possibilities.

The younger generations may not believe this, but back in the year 2000, shopping online was a pretty daunting ordeal. So much so, that many people chose to avoid it, sticking instead to going to stores in person. People were especially reluctant to order shoes online without first trying them on. Which was a huge problem for online shoe retailer Zappos, as they didn't have any stores. So, what did they do? They started offering free delivery and returns on all orders. Initially, this move received backlash from shareholders, who believed it would be a catastrophe, leading to a loss of cash. Yet by focusing on the potential benefits, the leaders were able to stay the course. Consumers loved the idea so much that the business exploded, taking Zappos from the edge of bankruptcy to being a thriving company.

When it comes to creating momentum and results in your life, giving up on short-term thinking can have similar effects for you. But to start doing it, you have to look at the choices you make on two levels: daily micro-actions and bigger-picture decisions. Both are important, yet they need to be handled in different ways.

Getting on top of daily micro-actions

These are the regular, reoccurring, small decisions you make every day. On their own, they may not have huge implications, but when compounded, they can have a huge snowball effect. Things like properly planning your day, getting in that workout, avoiding that tough conversation, missing date night, etc. Acting on these links back to the first chapter of this book, because getting on top of small decisions will often come down to putting yourself at cause and taking responsibility for the actions you take. That's why, before you give in to what is fun, comfortable or pleasurable, stop and think about the bigger implications of that action. What else haven't you factored in? What might you lose in the long run if you make the easy choice now? And what might you gain in the long run if you make the harder choice instead?

Stopping to take a moment to think through what you're facing and putting the situation into perspective may be exactly what you need to realign yourself with what you're doing and why. This in itself can break the cycle of you taking impulsive actions or making choices that seem great in the moment, but that you regret later. It may also be the push you need to take an action you know you need to take but have been avoiding. As when you see everything you have to gain, it can make it far easier to push through whatever is holding you back. That's why adopting this mindset and perspective is all about holding yourself to a higher standard and making the tough choices, even when they're inconvenient, challenging or you simply don't want to. It is those tougher choices that in the long run will lead to bigger payoffs and far greater satisfaction.

With that in mind, I want to challenge you to stop for a moment and think about an easy or comfortable impulse you gave into this week. Maybe you delayed facing a tough conversation, spent time scrolling through the newsfeed instead of starting a project or made an excuse to your partner about why you needed to work late. Or maybe you got pizza instead of a healthy dinner or sat on the couch watching Netflix instead of hitting the gym.

Got one? The important thing to remember here is that, in isolation, these decisions may not be a big deal. The problem, however, is when they become repeated behaviors. Now, think about that impulse from earlier. What are the potential long-term repercussions of this action? Especially if you continue repeating it? Maybe it'll lead to earning less money, someone in your team continuing to be toxic, your health continuing to deteriorate or a breakdown in your relationship?

On the flip side, what benefits do you have to gain if you follow through with the tougher but more meaningful option next time you face this decision? And how can you remind yourself of the future benefits of taking that action, so that you actually do it?

Sometimes just putting these decisions into perspective may be exactly what you need to break through the mental block of short-term thinking. That's why a good rule to live by is to always push yourself towards facing the painful action rather than the comfortable one. I know it's not easy, and at the time you may not enjoy or want to do it. But when you start approaching life and the choices you make in this way, you'll create a huge momentum shift in your thoughts, actions and decisions, which ultimately will directly affect your income, success and freedom.

Preparing for long-term goals

The second level of choices you make comes down to looking at the bigger picture and ensuring what you do is aligned with where you want to get to. Which means you need to know your goals and where you are going.

When it comes to goal setting and execution, I find that most people fall into one of three scenarios. The first is when they sit down once a year and set some goals because they feel like it's something they *should* do...then life happens, and they rarely think or look back at those goals. The second is when people get so caught up in their big vision of where they want to be in five years, that they don't know where to begin with setting goals or targets. *So they never start in the first place.* And lastly, despite knowing their goals, people get so pulled into life, responsibilities and daily challenges, that they don't get the time to work on the goals they set months ago.

The reality is that none of these approaches are ever going to lead to any real level of growth. That's why I'm not a big fan of 12-month goals. Sure, it's great to have an idea of where you want to be a year from now. But the problem is that 12 months is a long time and there are so many variables that simply can't be accounted for. Take the pandemic, for example. Most people set their New Year's resolutions like usual in 2020. Out of nowhere, the world was derailed, completely disrupting everything, including our plans and intentions. Add to that the fact that people also overestimate what they can do in a year. It's easy to build up this huge vision in your mind about what you want. What's not so easy is figuring out how long it will take or how much capacity you have to make it happen. This can lead to unrealistic expectations, which sets you up for failure and disappointment from the beginning.

Now don't get me wrong, setting 12-month goals can still be helpful, and it is something you should do. However, I believe you need to take it a step further and break those goals down into 90-day targets. These targets then become tangible, as you can set real outcomes and objectives, which are also easier to measure and adapt along the way.

The way I recommend thinking about goal setting is to:

1. Get clear on where you want to be 12 months from now.
2. Reverse engineer the journey, figuring out where you'd need to be in 90 days, to be on track for your 12 months goal to be achieved.
3. Break that down into your focus for the next seven days.
4. Every week, take some time to think about your progress and what you need to focus on for the next seven days, to continue moving forward.
5. Repeat and adapt, adjusting what you are doing whenever necessary.
6. Then, every quarter, reassess the next 90-day goals and set new objectives.

Regardless of whether it's a business, health or life goal, this system works because it allows you to take your macro vision and break it down into micro focuses. Every week, you will know exactly what to focus on in order to continue progressing. This is how you ensure that you keep momentum and stay focused, without getting lost in the bigger vision of what you are trying to achieve. Knowing this will also make it far easier to break the cycle of giving into short-term actions, since now your short-term actions are either aligned with your current seven-day focus or they aren't!

I use this way of thinking daily to ensure that the actions and choices I make are taking me towards my goals, not away from them. For instance: two of my biggest loves in life are fitness... and cake. Obviously, those two things don't work together well. That's why whenever I'm tempted to have a slice of cake, I can look at my focus for that week and whether or not the sacrifice is worth it. If I have a specific fitness target in mind, the short-term satisfaction of eating a piece of cake (especially if done regularly) could potentially derail my progress. So even though I may really want that cake, I can make a judgment call that it's not worth it—a decision which becomes even easier when I remind myself that 15 minutes later the cake will be gone, the enjoyment will be over and all I'll be left with is more work before I'm able to reach my goals.

Here's the best part though: when you follow this way of thinking, on the times you do decide to give in and enjoy life, you can do so guilt-free, as you've made a decision that it is what you want. Meaning it was a conscious choice, instead of an impulsive action.

This is why knowing your goals and taking the time to consider how your in-the-moment actions affect them is so important. This way of thinking is a key component of finding happiness and balance, as it puts you back in control of the choices you make and how you choose to live your life. In turn, this shift breaks the cycle of you simply living in the moment and frees you from the negative feelings and emotions that come with you regretting the actions you do or don't take.

What about really big decisions?

Whenever you're faced with a big decision, such as changing job, buying a house, launching a business or taking an action with huge life or financial implications, then rather than just focusing on the crucial action, it's essential to take time to break down all the future implications that could come as a result of that decision.

I've found the easiest way to do this is to write it down. Put the decision at the top of the page and then create two columns. On the left side write *"if I do this, what will happen?"* On the right side write *"if I don't do this, what will happen?"* What this will do is allow you to see the situation holistically and look at both what you have to gain, as well as potentially sacrifice by taking the action. So you don't get caught up in short-term micro actions here, make sure you ask these questions multiple times. Don't just stop with the next thing that might happen, consider what will potentially occur after that. And what about after that? Keep digging until you know the potential final outcome, or you have broken down what could happen, as far into the future as you can. This practice will allow you to create an outline of all the future potential implications, which will then give you the clarity you need to make a decision on what to do next. It will also keep you from potentially making the wrong decision due to not looking far enough ahead.

This happened to me early on in my entrepreneurial journey. My coaching business was struggling and after 18 months I'd made very little progress, even though I'd been working relentlessly, putting in 14-hour days, hustling and grinding to try and *make it happen*. The problem though, was I didn't really know what I was doing. So most of my days were pretty much just spent winging it, making it up as I went along and hoping I'd eventually figure out what works. Hope, however, is not a strategy, and not only was I running out of money, but the days of feeling like I was banging my head against the wall and not making progress were also more and more frequent, causing a huge amount of stress. I reached a point where I knew that if I was going to make this happen, then I was going to need help. There was a company I'd been following that supported businesses exactly like mine, and I believed they would give me the right support to turn this around. After reaching out to them though, I found out that getting help would cost $10,000. I remember just freezing at the amount. It was more than I could fathom, and way more than I had, especially with how badly I'd been doing revenue-wise.

Now, if I just stopped at considering the initial action—which was parting with all that money—clearly it would seem like far too big of a risk and the wrong decision. That was why it was essential to look at both sides of the issue, as I needed to get a clearer picture of what the results of that decision could be.

By diving deeper into what would happen if I didn't take this action, I could see the future reality I was facing. After 18 months of struggling on my own and being unable to get it right, it was only a matter of time until I had to throw in the towel. That in itself would mean quitting the business and going back to the corporate world to work on someone else's dreams instead of my own, which was the very situation I'd been so miserable in and worked so hard to get away from. On the other side though, taking this action could mean finally figuring out what I needed to do to bring in more clients and build a business that could provide for me financially. All of which would allow me to finally find the fulfillment and impact I wanted, all while relieving me of the huge amount of stress I was under.

This is why it is so important to fully break down the potential future outcomes of what *could* happen. Without doing so, I could have easily focused on the pain that came with the initial action (in this case, the potential risk and parting with cash I didn't have). When I compared the two potential realities, suddenly I could see that the potential pain of not following through far outweighed my fear of what could go wrong. With all of this in front of me, I knew I had to find a way to hire this company. In the end, I got a loan to fund their fee—and if I hadn't, you probably wouldn't be reading this book today.

Now, I want to be clear. Nothing in life is guaranteed and despite all the potential benefits, there was no certainty my decision would pay off. However, in this situation, my decision was calculated. I'd done my research and due diligence, and I'd gathered all the information I needed to be as certain as I could be that this was the right path. For me, the potential reward was far greater than the risk.

It's also important to note that while I was making this decision, people around me told me I was crazy. Understandably so, since they didn't know my goals, vision or reasons why I needed to do this. Because of that, they were just focused on the financial risk and blinded to the potential benefits that came with it. That's why when it comes to giving up on short-term thinking, you need to ensure your focus isn't swayed by other people. Sure, get input and guidance, but always remember where it's coming from and don't allow the doubts, fears or self-imposed limitations of others to hold you back from what you need to do. Especially if they don't know the full story.

The important thing to realize here is that when it comes to big decisions, just focusing on the immediate action will almost always seem like the wrong decision. Especially since you'll usually be focusing on what you're sacrificing or have to lose. This is why whenever you're making big decisions, it's essential that you consider *both* the potential gains and potential repercussions of what could happen, as that's how you'll see the full context of the situation.

The truth about short-term thinking

Everyone wants success, financial freedom, to be in shape and to have fulfillment in their lives. The unfortunate reality though is that very few people are willing to do what it takes to create the life that they want. That's why if you want to live a life that others never will, then you have to be willing to take the actions others won't.

This is where giving up on short-term thinking comes in. This mindset and way of approaching choices in your life is how you'll be able to separate yourself from those who will never reach their potential. After all, those who are willing to settle for average can get away with focusing on feeling comfortable in the moment. If you want to live an extraordinary life and to become the best version of yourself though, you have to approach life differently. That means you have to hold yourself to a higher standard, where you give up on in-the-moment actions based on instant gratification, opting instead for choices that get you closer to where you want to be.

Obviously, that doesn't mean never stop and enjoy life. It does, however, mean that you'll need to start being more intentional. As we saw earlier in this chapter, achieving your goals or creating the life you want will often mean that you'll have to prioritize what you want most over what you want right now. When you start to think this way and view decisions in this light, it will open you up to a whole new world of possibilities that before was limited only by your level of thinking. Instead of allowing your in-the-moment actions to sabotage your long-term growth, you will be able to reach new levels of success that before you could have only imagined.

I know it's not easy, especially when you're in tough spots or challenged with huge life-changing decisions. In these moments, knowing all the consequences and potential outcomes might not be enough, and can still leave you afraid of taking action. I get it completely, and I know how terrifying following through with what you know you need to do can be. That's why there is one more strategy you can use to mentally ensure you are in the right state of mind: *stop and imagine that you've already achieved your goals.*

Think ahead and get a mental image of what you want your new reality to be. Visualize yourself having lost the weight, grown your business, achieved that promotion, etc. Then with that in mind, pull your focus back into your present situation and ask yourself: *what would that future me do right now?*

By doing this, you can take who you are and your current reality out of the equation, and instead, base your decision on what the person you want to become would do in that situation. For instance, let's say you need to have a tough conversation that could massively alter the trajectory of your life. The current version of you may be focused too much on the short-term pain to face it. But if you think ahead to the end of your 90-day goals and the person you'd become, what would that person do?

Would they freeze and put it off? Or would they face it head on, as they know it needs to be done?

The same way of thinking goes for every situation you find yourself in. Whether it's putting out a video, starting a business, hiring a mentor, leaving a toxic relationship, or whatever tough call you find yourself in. Think ahead to a future point in time when you've achieved your goals, and figure out what that version of you would have done to make them a reality. Then use that clarity to push yourself to take that action. The purpose of thinking bigger is to start making decisions based on where you are trying to get to, not just on where you are. Because, don't forget, achieving amazing success takes hard work and sacrifice, so you will at times need to give up what you want right now for what you want long-term. Start doing this regularly, and you'll see a huge shift, not just in your results, but in your confidence and how you feel about yourself.

Giving priority to instant gratification in the context of your long-term goals will only add weight to your bag of rocks. Remember going forward, giving up on short-term thinking is essential for you to achieve the life you want and to become the person you've always wanted to be. Drop this rock to make your bag lighter and your journey easier.

CHAPTER 4

Maybe you should give up...
fixating on the future

—=—

S hort-term thinking can be a big problem—and as we've now seen, the way to give up on it is to focus on long-term thinking. While this mentality will go a long way towards helping you make better decisions and achieve your goals, focusing too much on the future can also bring with it many problems you need to watch out for. These include:

1. Focusing too much on what *will* go wrong.
2. Making up future problems of how things *might* go wrong.
3. Fixating on where you're *going* rather than the present.

All three of these can cause you to get stuck in your own head, to the point where all your time and energy get wasted on things that are out of your control. Not only can this derail your progress, it can also cause a whirlwind of anxiety and stress. That's why fixating on the future needs to be the next big rock that you let go of on this journey of getting out of your own way. If you don't, it'll push you back a step to one of the earlier areas of this book, where you'll get stuck in a world of effect, become controlled by fear or make short-sighted decisions that come at the expense of your long-term success. While we don't want to abandon long-term thinking, we need to make sure we're doing it in a healthy and strategic way. By giving up fixating on the future as either a scary place where everything will go wrong or a heavenly place that will solve all your problems for you, you'll be able to use your new long-term thinking skills without trapping yourself in emotion.

To be clear, unless you become completely numb to the world around you, you're probably never going to be able to fully stop worrying about your potential future problems. After all, no one can predict the future, and there will always be an element of uncertainty as you move towards your goals. But that doesn't mean you can't reduce the negative feelings that come from fixating on the future.

Focusing too much on what will go wrong

We all have a tendency to get caught up in worrying about future problems that we might have to deal with. It's completely understandable, especially when you have big challenges, responsibilities or issues that could potentially turn life upside down. When you lie in bed at night worrying about where your next client is going to come from or how if you don't solve that business challenge you may get fired, you're experiencing real and valid concerns. So I know that telling you to simply stop worrying about these future problems is useless advice. Because if it was that easy, you'd have done it already.

As a business owner running a 150-staff global production company, Alan had his hands full with the repercussions brought on by the pandemic, regulatory changes and the great resignation. Highly dependent on manual labor, it meant his business was going through an incredibly turbulent time. Not only were they having issues implementing new legislation, they also had challenges hiring the right staff, delivering for customers, making payroll and a whole host of other challenges. I'm sure you can imagine that this was a huge amount of pressure, and it often meant that Alan was facing sleepless nights worrying about keeping the lights on, clients happy, compliance satisfied and paychecks coming to 150 families who were depending on him. Alan's worries were completely legitimate, as there was a huge chance they could turn into reality. So simply ignoring them, sweeping them under the rug or pretending they weren't there wasn't going to help. In fact, doing so would just make the situation worse.

The problem he faced, though, was that he was so focused on how bad the outcome would be if he didn't handle these issues, that he wasn't focusing on figuring out a solution or doing something to turn it around. All of which created a vicious cycle where the worries led to more stress and aggravation, causing even more sleepless nights.

Now obviously, you need to be aware of future problems you'll likely encounter in your life. Being oblivious, willfully ignorant or overly optimistic about the future can leave you unprepared and more likely to be blindsided by these issues. However, knowing what the potential issues are and then doing something to avoid or prepare for them is a completely different action than sitting around worrying about how they could turn out.

That's why Alan needed to stop focusing so much on the huge catastrophe that would happen in six months if he didn't fix these problems. Instead, he needed to pull his energy into the present and focus on what he could do today to solve these issues. While this didn't make the worry completely go away, it did allow him to take back some control. Rather than just spending his days fixated on how bad things could turn out, he was able to empower himself to take action on turning the situation around.

Someone once said if you stress about something before it happens, you essentially put yourself through it twice—once when it actually happens and once ahead of time. If you want to feel more in control of handling problems, you need to give up on focusing so much on how awful the problem will be and instead start focusing on what you can do about it. After all, the problem is going to be there regardless, so going back to cause and effect, you have the ability to choose how you respond to it. I've found that in order to do that, the most powerful question you can use during those times is "what do I need to do about this?"

This simple question is so powerful because it pulls your focus from the future into the present. In the future, a potential problem has already happened and it's too late to do anything about it. But in the present, it hasn't happened yet! You can use your time now to prepare for it and figure out the actions you'll need to take if it does happen, or better yet, take action now to help make sure it doesn't.

This idea applies to every situation of your life, whether you are worried about losing your job, having a breakdown in your marriage, your health deteriorating further or letting down those around you. For instance, if you are worried about running out of money, instead of focusing on the idea that you might have to fold your business or that you'll be unable to pay your rent, think of what you can do to boost your income. Do you need to spend more time generating customers? Find an additional stream of revenue? Pivot what you do to solve a bigger or more relevant problem? Create a side hustle that brings in more cash? Or let's say you are worried about a potential breakdown in your relationship. To prevent this from happening, maybe you need to set better boundaries with work, hire more support around the house or reorganize your life to make your relationship a priority.

This practice isn't removing the problem from your awareness, or even removing your apprehension about it. Instead, it's changing your perspective and putting your focus on what you need to do to fix the problem when it happens. This is key, as a lot of people know the potential consequences of inaction but still don't do anything to solve the situation. This is why it is so important to figure out what you want and your potential solutions, and then focus on what you need to do instead of delaying.

Making up future problems that might go wrong

Whether it's in life, business, your goals, responsibilities or whatever else you have going on, you will encounter problems and setbacks—it's inevitable, and part of the journey. The reality, though, is that we as human beings are really good at thinking those problems are *always about to happen to us*. Remember how our brains are wired to keep us safe at all costs? This wiring leads us to make assumptions, jump to conclusions, blow issues out of proportion, and generally believe that the sky is falling any time something doesn't go exactly the way we think it should.

Matthew was his own worst enemy when it came to this reaction. His business had recently hit a few large setbacks and lost a portion of their funding. One morning he called me in a panic. He said he'd just gotten a call from one of his remaining investors, who had requested a sit-down meeting with him and the other founders. This had never happened before, and Matthew was convinced it was because the investor was going to drop them. I forced him to pull himself back into the present moment and recognize he had no way of knowing that for certain. The reality was that there were so many different ways this situation could play out, yet he was convincing himself the story in his head was the only way it could end. We took a moment to look at all the scenarios and ways in which this situation could go, many of which were actually positive. Even though doing this didn't magically solve the problem, what it did do was allow him to calm down and put himself at ease. Later that day he and his partners attended the meeting and it turned out that despite the bad news, the investor still loved what they were doing and he wanted to know how else he could help. So instead of it being some huge tragedy, it was a positive experience. Yet because he was so convinced it would be a disaster, prior to this meeting Matthew had worked himself into a rollercoaster of unnecessary stress.

This is a reaction I see in a lot of the people I work with, where at the first sign of trouble they immediately focus on how everything is about to come crashing down. And I bet you do it, too. Like if your boss or client asks to speak to you and your immediate thought is that you are going to get fired, when it's just an update on a new project. Or you receive a doctor's letter and you immediately freak out that something is wrong, when it's just a reminder for a routine check-up. Or your partner is upset so you worry about what you did, when really, they're just tired or had a stressful day at work.

In all of these situations, you're literally making up stories. You have no guarantee or very little evidence that what you're afraid of will actually happen. But because you build it up so much in your head, that story feels like a reality, where disaster is inevitable.

Whenever you find yourself focusing on future problems, worrying about what will happen, or feeling like everything is about to fall apart, pull yourself back into the present. Stop and think about whether you know this for certain. As in, is this outcome a fact, guaranteed or definitely going to happen? Or is it just a story in your head? Once you know that it's just a story, take some time to put the situation into perspective. How else could this play out? What else could be going on? What other outcomes might happen—and might some of them be more positive than the one you're predicting? Then from there, consider what might even go *right* in this scenario? Doing this may not make all the worry go away, but it will allow you to reduce the stress that comes with seeing a terrible outcome as inevitable. Sometimes just knowing there are alternative outcomes or seeing the situation for what it truly is will be exactly what you need to feel more grounded.

Not only that, but by slowing down and putting the problem into perspective, you'll also be able to see that even if it does go wrong, chances are it's hardly the end of the world, or at least, nowhere near as big of a catastrophe as you were building up in your head. Plus, you already know how to handle the problems that *will* happen to you from the previous chapter, so focus on what you can control and what you need to do about it.

If you want to stop worrying so much about potential future problems, then you have to catch yourself in the act of making up doomsday stories that have no evidence of actually coming true. This is how you'll stop fixating so much on the future, as instead, you bring your focus into the present and the situation at hand.

Fixating on where you're *going* rather than the present

Do you ever work really hard to reach a goal, actually achieve that goal, start to celebrate, and then feel…numb? Like something is missing and it wasn't actually what you thought you wanted? You know you should be excited, but for some reason, you just aren't. Next thing you know, you start thinking about your *next* goal, completely forgetting about the one you just worked so hard to reach. I see this happen all the time with my clients. I've also done this countless times myself as well. Everything from huge business milestones to conquering health goals all seem to end with a feeling of "is that it?" I've come to call this the "curse of the high achiever", as no accomplishment seems to fill that internal void or live up to their expectations.

The reason this happens is simple: *you are never going to get to where you want to be.* As soon as you get close to it, the goal post will move and you'll start pushing towards the next level, the next goal, the next milestone. That's why what you achieve never feels like it's enough. You're so focused on the future that you become frustrated and disheartened that you're not doing enough or aren't further along. Like if you lose 10 pounds, yet feel like it's nothing as you still aren't at your goal weight. Or you land that new client, yet dismiss the win as it hasn't got you to your yearly sales quota. This fixation on the future is taking your focus away from the present and dismissing what you accomplished. Instead, you become consumed by the thought of what you have yet to achieve. No wonder it never feels like enough.

Does that mean you're destined to live a life of feeling empty and unfulfilled? Or that you need to just stop chasing your dreams? Of course not. What it does mean though is that you need to shift how you view those dreams and goals.

Turning this around starts with having an actual plan of where you are going, so you can use the present as your path to the future rather than just staring into the future as the present slips by.

I speak to people all the time who tell me that they want to start a business, write a book, train for an event, lose weight—yet when I ask how far along they are, it's still something they're just thinking about. Sometimes they've been thinking about it for years and still haven't begun! These people are so caught up in the vision of what they want in the future, that instead of feeling motivated and taking action in the present, they feel overwhelmed and don't do anything. This is another big reason you may be fixating on potential problems or making up disaster stories—when you're overwhelmed just by the possibility of doing something, it's really easy to envision it going wrong!

Here's the thing though—most of the time when someone tells me they're *OVERwhelmed*, they're actually *UNDERplanned*.

Think about it. Whether you're completing a project at work, going on vacation, or starting a fitness routine, how much easier is it to do it when you have a plan? When you've taken the time to process all your thoughts, organize your tasks, get clarity around your goals and set up a blueprint to follow, the whole endeavor feels lighter.

This probably sounds obvious, but you'd be surprised how many people don't take the time to figure out what they need to do. Instead, they either dive right in hoping for the best, or they just keep thinking about what they want but never do anything to make it happen. Both of those are future-fixation traps, as they assume that the future will solve all potential problems for them. Don't fall for these traps!

The first step in making a workable plan is to figure out your desired end result. To make this happen, you have two ways you can approach it: either reverse engineer it or figure out the very first step:

1. Reverse-engineer it

Start at the end and work backward. What's the end goal? What else needs to happen before, to enable that end goal to happen?

For instance, let's say you want to start putting out video content. In this case, the end result would be posting your first video. With that in mind, you can then figure out the steps in between. That may mean the step before is uploading the video, and the step before is filming, the step before is writing a script. If it's easier or clearer for you, you can also start by figuring out the end result. With that in mind, you can then figure out what the first step would be and then fill out all the other steps from there. By doing this you'll be able to uncover all the actions you need to take. As you work your way through, you may even figure out aspects you overlooked. Like with the video, you may realize when you look at the plan, something you missed out was editing what you filmed.

Regardless of the goal, the process will be the same, and by taking the time to do this, you'll gain clarity on exactly what needs to get done and what your milestones are. You'll also have a starting point, with a clear step-by-step plan to get to where you want to be.

Sometimes though, it's not that simple, especially if it's a venture you don't know how to approach or there are too many variables or unknowns in between to map it all out. In that case, the second thing you can do is:

2. Knowing the end result, figure out what is the first step you need to take.

From there you can take the first action, after which you can reassess, keeping your end result in mind and then figure out what is next. Repeat until you either reach your goal, or you gain enough clarity to put together a more concise plan. This way you're pinning down variables one at a time, which will enable you to take better-informed actions in the future.

This process is helpful because most people are focusing on step five instead of where they need to begin. It's like if you wanted to run a marathon, but for the last few years, you've been inactive. Of course focusing on the marathon will seem terrifying! When you break it down though and just focus on step one, which may be going out for a first jog, then it becomes far less daunting. Not only that, but it also seems achievable and something you can do. It's the same for every other goal you want to achieve. Instead of focusing on getting ten new clients, focus on what you need to do to close the first one. Instead of focusing on losing 50 pounds, focus on your first day of eating healthier. Whatever it is, break it down into a micro step, as that will allow you to feel far more confident in making it happen.

The best part about this approach is that you can repeat the process to create a plan for whatever you want to do with your life. Whether your goal is in business, fitness, finances or anything else you want to achieve, the way to figure out what to do is the same.

Having a clear plan also solves another problem—it makes what you are doing far more manageable, so you're less likely to feel overwhelmed or get preoccupied with problems you might run into.

Once you have a plan in place, it's essential to track your progress along the way. After all, we normalize what we repeatedly do, which is why once you overcome the problems you have today, chances are a few weeks from now you'll have forgotten they were even an issue. This again can cause you to lose sight of how far you've come, leading to further frustration and feelings that you should be further along.

One way to avoid this is to keep a record of your progress. You can do this in three ways. You can write down where you are, how you feel and what you want to achieve at the start of the process. Or, every week you can take some time to reflect on what you achieved and what was moved forward. Thirdly, you can keep a record of all your wins (which often if you don't stop to think about them will be missed or overlooked).

The way I recommend approaching this is to keep a journal that you add to along the way. It doesn't need to take long, and you could either set aside a couple of minutes each day or at the end of each week to reflect on what happened and what you did. I like doing it daily because it's easier to do when it's fresh in your mind, especially since a lot can happen in a week, making it easy to forget. There's no right or wrong though, as it's all about figuring out how you prefer to do it, what adds to your life and most importantly, what you can be consistent with.

By keeping these records, you'll have something tangible you can then revisit to remind yourself how far you have come. You'll also be able to use these insights to figure out the next steps and what you need to focus on going forward.

Remember what you've been through

There's one more helpful strategy for giving up on fixating on the future that I want to share with you: remember you've been here before. Your past and present used to be your future. Regardless of the setbacks you've faced in your life, you've survived 100% of your worst days and you're still here fighting. Even in the times you felt trapped and saw no hope, where you didn't know whether or not you'd survive, you reading this right now shows that you did. So whatever challenges you may be facing, even if it doesn't feel like it, you will make it through them too. Even if things do fall apart and the worst does happen, you can and will find a way to turn it around. It may not happen overnight, and it may be incredibly hard to do so, but somehow, someway, you will get back on your feet.

I know that in the moment that may not ease the struggles you are facing or make anything better. But sometimes just knowing and reminding yourself of how strong you truly are can make the future feel far more manageable. This in itself is also why it's so important to remember that life is a journey, not a race. And along the way, not everything will always go according to plan. You will make mistakes, fall off track and you will mess up. And that's okay! When you pull your focus into the present, you can view these setbacks as minor inconveniences rather than major catastrophes, which will make it far easier to refocus and carry on with what you are doing. After all, a bad day in isolation may feel like the end of the world, when actually, a few bad days in the bigger picture of a year or a decade are nothing. It only becomes a big deal when you build it up in your head as one. Recognizing this can remove a huge amount of pressure, especially since those feelings of frustration and discouragement are largely down to expectations that you're placing on yourself.

This is why perspective and how you choose to look at what is happening is so important. Because when you just fixate on the future, it can cause you to spend your life feeling like you are miles away from where you want to be—while completely overlooking the fact that you are miles away from where you began! That's why it's so important to slow down, recognize how far you've come and remind yourself of everything you've achieved along the way.

Here's what I want you to remember: right here and now, you are in the middle of what you used to want. I'll say that again as I want this to fully sink in. **Right here and now, you are in the middle of what you used to want.**

It's so easy to forget that a year ago you desperately wanted to be where you are right now. When you take a step back and remember that, it's actually pretty amazing, right?

The reality is that happiness and fulfillment don't come from the end result somewhere in the future. Instead, they come from the journey, and the journey takes place in the present. When you learn to view your progress in this light, then it doesn't matter if or when your goals change, the goal post moves or you run into problems. Now, your happiness and growth will come from improvement and progression, rather than achievement.

Another way to look at this is to remember that we're all going to die. I know that sounds morbid, but that realization in itself can often put life and your everyday problems into perspective. Especially when you remind yourself how amazing the fact that you're here right now truly is. Just being aware of that can be a great reminder of what is truly important, particularly during times when you feel overwhelmed by your problems. Often framing those moments within the bigger picture can be exactly what you need to see that they're either not that big of a deal, or are something that you can handle and get through.

At the end of the day, life is a lot longer than you realize, yet because people put so much pressure on themselves to get to where they want to be, they miss out on the process. Or they get so caught up in their problems, that they overlook the positives of the present they're in. Chances are though that what you fixate on today, you'll probably have forgotten tomorrow. And when you realize that, it'll make it far easier to let the future go so that you can enjoy the time that you have today.

If you want to find joy in your achievements and appreciate the journey, then you have to give up on fixating on the future. That's the only way you will be able to fully enjoy the present.

CHAPTER 5

Maybe you should give up...
comparing yourself to others

—=—

"*Comparison is the thief of joy.*" You've probably heard that saying a few times, but it's worth repeating. Because nothing will sabotage your happiness faster than comparing your life, what you have or what you are doing to other people.

The problem with comparing yourself to others is that it places your focus on what you feel like you are lacking, rather than on what you're doing well, what you've achieved or even what you want. This reinforces the story in your head that you'll never have or be enough, as someone else will always have more than you. As a result, you fixate on earning more money because you don't have as much as your friend who just got a promotion. You fixate on losing more weight because you don't have a six-pack like that guy on the beach. You start to doubt your relationship because you feel like it isn't straight out of a movie. Worst of all, you start to feel that any progress you might be making isn't enough, especially when you're constantly reminded that everyone else is so much further ahead.

This in itself is one of the reasons why so many people are never able to be truly happy. After all, it's difficult to feel joy or fulfillment when many of your choices and decisions in life are driven by the desire to fill the gaps you think you're missing.

If you don't give up on comparing yourself to others, then no matter what you achieve, *you will never feel like it's enough.* In fact, you won't even see the journey you're on for what it is—as a path to improving your own life—you'll just see it as a never-ending chase to get what everyone else has.

This outlook has several problems. First, often what you think or feel you want isn't actually a real desire of yours—instead, it was placed in your head by the endless barrage of advertising you see every day. Second, what everyone else has, usually isn't as great as it looks. Third, even if those things make *those* people happy, there's no guarantee that they'll make *you* happy. And finally, getting those things might not even be possible for you—or might not be worth the price you pay to get them. Let's start with the first issue.

What ads want you to want

It seems like everywhere you look these days you're bombarded with images and stories about what the perfect body, relationship and life look like. They're literally everywhere— on TV, in magazines or even at bus stops and plastered on walls around the subway. From the outside, all this advertising may seem harmless, but when you look closer, you'll see that every bit of it is about what you're missing or what you need to have a better life. And whether you realize it or not, on a subconscious level these constant reminders are designed to get you to compare your own life to some make-believe reality, reinforcing the idea in your head that you're missing out on something or that you're not enough.

From a profit and sales standpoint, it's pretty genius. There's a reason why advertising is a multibillion-dollar industry. Our dreams (and insecurities) feed it. And to make it all work, it's filled with people whose primary focus is to convince you and me to part ways with our cash to create this fairy-tale life they've managed to sell us. And they've gotten so good at it, that the vast majority of the time we won't even realize it's happening.

I remember back when I was trying to lose weight and get in shape, I'd spend so much money on supplements in the hope I'd finally get that Instagram-ready body of my dreams. One time in particular, during a trip to a health store, the eager clerk sold me some fat burners from a stand using images of guys with six-packs in its marketing—the exact look I was striving for. The guy helping me with my purchase looked like he lived in the gym, which was why his entire sales pitch of how throughout my workouts I'd be *melting fat right off* was so convincing. It sounded amazing and like this would transform my body, so I left that store excited, with two bottles in hand and ready to start *shredding fat*. As you can probably guess…that didn't happen. Instead, all I got was a $50 upset stomach.

Looking back, I can see now that a huge part of the problem was my incessant need to compare my progress to other people. As I looked around the gym and on Instagram, I was faced with a constant reminder that someone else was leaner than I was. That someone else had bigger arms. That someone else was *"insert whatever else I felt insecure about on that day"*. It's no wonder that internally I felt like I still wasn't enough, and that

I needed to do whatever I could to get leaner faster...even if I knew it sounded too good to be true. That's why I'd look for shortcuts or ways to speed up the process. All of which made me a perfect target for advertisers and salespeople.

This doesn't just happen in products we hope will solve our problems. Instead, it can come into play in everyday goods that you wouldn't think twice about. Just look around the supermarket. Most food brands have advertising on them, building up an idea in your mind about what your life will look like if you buy or use their product.

I even saw this recently on the packaging for some yogurt, where they had included a picture of a happy family eating breakfast together. From the outside it seems harmless—you wouldn't even think about it, especially when you're in a rush. On a subliminal level though, this packaging is designed to get you to compare your life to the image, convincing you that if you buy their product, you too will have that happy family morning. Like I said, very clever stuff, especially when the advertisers know that on a subconscious level, the emotional response you feel can be what causes you to buy their product over a competitor's.

The problem though is that this is something you're continuously exposed to throughout the day. In fact, unless you become a recluse in the woods disowning all technology, it's almost impossible to avoid. Which is why it's no surprise that most people live their lives in a comparison trap, constantly focusing on what is missing. To make matters worse, they're oblivious to it even going on. Instead, all they feel is that something is missing, especially since whatever they are doing doesn't live up to their expectations of what the perfect life looks like in their head.

But advertising isn't the only problem here, it's only one piece of the puzzle. If we're going to talk about comparison being the thief of joy, we also have to talk about social media.

Keeping up with...everyone on social media

I don't know about you, but as a kid, I used to view being forced to sit down and look at someone else's holiday photos as a punishment. It was boring and tedious to try and fake interest in something I didn't care about—especially since I wasn't there and it had nothing to do with me.

Now though, we all put ourselves through this exact torment every day. You know how it goes: you're sitting there in your underwear trying to get up for work, and on your social media app of choice you see Jenny is on her dream holiday in the Maldives. Scroll down and you see Brad is cramming in another 6 AM workout. Scroll down more, and you see more of the same—other people living exciting, productive or glamorous lives. Meanwhile, you're sitting there on the couch eating your bowl of corn flakes for the 138th day in a row, you can't help but feel that in comparison, your life is blah and boring. It can leave you feeling like there's something wrong with you—because if you were as great as you should be, you'd have a life as awesome as Jenny or Brad.

The worst part of all this is that often you don't even realize how much you're hurting yourself. Especially since scrolling through social media is such a habit for just about everyone. By design, it's addictive. Just think, whether you're watching TV, avoiding work, or standing in a queue at the supermarket, how often do you pull out your phone and start scrolling? Chances are, the answer is far more than you realize, as most of the time, we do it out of habit without even recognizing or thinking about it.

Not only that, but we also don't ever stop to consider just how unrealistic social media portrayals actually are. The reality is that people only show you what they want you to see. Meaning you're essentially comparing your full life to someone else's highlight reel. So of course what you are doing will seem less exciting. After all, highlight reels are only the best bits. They leave out everything else—like the mundane, the negative or the reasons behind someone's actions. Jenny could have maxed out that credit card to pay for that trip. Brad could be going to the gym first thing to avoid facing another argument with his wife. Emily could have taken 205 selfies to capture the one perfect angle where she's happy with her look. You never truly know, which is why you need to recognize that all of these pictures have been chosen by design, to illustrate only what people are willing to share.

The reality is that you have no clue what is going on in their head or behind closed doors, which is why it's so important to make sure you're not jumping to conclusions or making assumptions about what you're seeing. Especially when that comparison leads to you feeling bad about yourself and your perception of how your life compares to everyone else's.

That in itself brings us to the next point—what other people have might not be what you want.

Do you really want what you want?

I remember when I first started my business a few of my friends were doing pretty well in their careers. They'd gotten several promotions and had reached the point where they were buying their first houses and settling down. I, on the other hand, was still renting and single. I started to feel like I was behind everyone else and not where I should be at this point in my life. That feeling of being *behind* caused a huge amount of frustration, causing me to start doubting what I was doing and whether or not I was making a mistake and on the wrong path.

One day though, I realized—I didn't want what they had. I didn't want that kind of career. I didn't want to work for someone else. I didn't want to be young and tied to a mortgage or have kids. Instead, I wanted my own business, to work my own hours and to have the freedom I desired. It was only when I brought this into my awareness that I could see I was beating myself up for no reason. After all, comparing myself to people whose goals and desires didn't even align with mine was ridiculous. It was only when I accepted that my friends' goals and my goals were different, that I could let it go.

That's the problem when you compare your life to others; often you'll build up stories in your head convincing yourself that you want something that you actually don't. I saw this come up in a conversation with a client who, after years of hard work advancing her career, she bought a designer handbag that cost more money than she earned in a month at the start of her career. Lauren told me about how she had yearned for this bag for years. For her, it was a status symbol, a sign to show that she made it. Yet within a few hours of buying it, she still felt empty. In the end, Lauren decided to return the bag, as she realized that not only was it crazy to spend that much money on it, it also did nothing to improve her self-worth or how she felt about herself.

This is why it's so important to stop and think about what you truly want in life. Do you want what your best friend has because you truly want it? Or are you unclear about what you actually want? Or afraid to admit to yourself that you want something different? Do you want something because it really brings you joy, or because you hope it will fill a void?

I know that these are tough questions to answer. Especially since what you think you want may have been ingrained in you from a young age. Parental pressure to take a certain job or career path, to have a big wedding, to follow the *"right"* religion or to own a particular kind of house is a very real thing. And a lot of people accept these paths or allow their lives to be determined by cultural or societal norms. This, in itself, can make you feel like you're having to face an internal battle—doing whatever is expected of you versus doing what you feel is true to you. Not only is it stressful, but it can also cause you to spend your days living for others, rather than creating a life that is true to yourself. That's why you are never going to be truly happy until you give up on comparing yourself to others or doing what's expected of you based on those cultural or societal norms (when they're not in alignment with who you are).

We've seen the effects of ads and social media on our self-expectations, and how we can be influenced to think that we want something we don't. Finally, let's now look at how detrimental it can be to want something that you actually can't get…or that might come at too high a cost.

Trying to emulate your heroes

It's easy to think that looking at really rich, famous or successful people for inspiration or motivation is a great idea. And sometimes it can be…but not always. I've had so many conversations with clients who place their heroes on a pedestal and truly believe that to be successful, they have to act and behave *exactly like them.*

I saw this with one client who idolized Elon Musk. Gareth would regularly watch Elon's speeches and motivational videos, which were a huge push for him to keep working towards his goals. And sure, it was great from a motivation standpoint, but after a while, it started to get toxic. See, Gareth had built up in his mind the idea that if Elon could run on four hours of sleep and work twenty-hour days, seven days a week, he needed to do that as well. As a result, he pushed himself to an extreme level of burnout, where the lack of sleep, self-care and recovery time nearly destroyed his life. He couldn't even remember the last time he took a day off and his doctors were concerned that he was heading for a heart attack. Despite knowing all this, Gareth still believed he needed to push through, as he felt guilty that he couldn't thrive on the same schedule that Elon Musk kept. Not being able to meet this imaginary standard had created a story in his head, where he believed that he was a failure who couldn't cut it.

That's the problem when you compare yourself to others. Whether it's your friends, your idols/heroes/mentors or simply people you see in ads, you create mental stories based on assumptions about the context of their lives (how good they have it, how easy it must be for them, how successful they are). Then you make decisions based on that false sense of reality— decisions that rarely help you, and often end up hurting you and your progress toward a better life. In other words, you sabotage yourself by trying to live up to something that often isn't even real (or at least not realistic for you).

Why comparison destroys happiness

Feelings of inadequacy run rampant in our lives when we compare ourselves to others—not just our heroes or our peers, but even our own future selves. Think of how many times you felt bad about yourself because you thought that you're not where you *should be* at this stage in your life.

I've had conversations with people who have amazing businesses, but feel like they failed as they aren't married or don't have kids yet. I've spoken to people excelling in their careers who still feel they're not doing good enough compared to a friend who got a promotion before they did. Or people who have had incredible health transformations, yet compared to a model on Instagram, they still feel they aren't good enough.

Daniel was a client of mine who had multiple promotions in his career. Yet despite his achievements, in one of our sessions, he broke down, telling me he felt like a failure, as compared to other people his age, he hadn't achieved enough. I stopped him in his tracks and asked him who he was comparing himself with. He went quiet for several minutes before he eventually blurted out *"Tim Ferriss"*.

Now if you don't know who Tim Ferriss is, you've probably heard of his best-selling book *The 4-Hour Work Week*. The book was a global hit, and it's completely understandable why this client looked up to Tim—Daniel also had a vision of reaching millions of people while doing work that he felt was having a positive impact on the world. However, comparing his level of success to Tim's was ludicrous. Especially since Tim is a one-in-a-billion success story—and like Elon Musk, lives a very extreme life. It was only when I pointed this out that my client realized how crazy what he was doing was. In the end, Daniel just laughed, especially since he couldn't even name anyone in his actual life who met that kind of standards either! Instead, he realized that this whole thing was just that sabotaging voice in his head going wild and making up stories based on his perception of where he felt he should be, leaving him feeling like he wasn't enough.

The thing is, *where you should be* is a completely made-up destination. There's no guide to life or set agenda that outlines what you should be doing at any given point. That entire pressure and rush to get to where you think you should be is stemming from the perception of what others are doing or how you've been told you should be living your life. That's the problem when you spend your life comparing yourself to everyone else. Because someone will always be in better shape. Someone will always have a bigger house or fancier car. Someone will always be earning more money. Someone will always be *"further along"* than you are. Which is why if you spend your days comparing yourself to those in front of you, it'll always feel like you're behind. Because of that, judging your happiness and life on those metrics is never going to lead to any form of joy or fulfillment, as no matter what you do, it'll always feel like who you are and what you have is never enough. So how do you give up on comparing yourself to other people?

How to give up on comparison

First things first, let's start with how *not* to. When it comes to escaping the comparison trap, probably the most common piece of advice is to practice gratitude and focus on all of the wonderful things going on in your life. And sure, being grateful helps, but how often do you know you *should* feel grateful for what you have…yet you still can't shake the feeling that something is missing, often resenting yourself and others or that you want more than you already have? This was a mental struggle I massively battled during a really dark period of my life. I knew with what I had and how life was going that I should be feeling great. And I could point to tons of things I was grateful for! But still, I wasn't happy. And knowing that just brought on huge feelings of guilt, which in turn, just made me feel even worse about myself. That's why as valuable as gratitude can be, I find that whenever one of those gurus spouts out advice to *just practice gratitude*, it just feels fluffy. Kind of like when someone says *"just love yourself"*. Sounds great in theory, but in reality, it doesn't really help.

Here's what really works for giving up on comparing yourself to others:

1. Determine where you're making comparisons and what triggers them.
2. Figure out what you want and what's important to you.
3. Focus on #2 so closely that it leaves no room for #1.

Finding your comparison triggers

When we fall into a comparison trap, it typically doesn't happen by accident. Something triggers that emotional response— usually something very specific.

My client Martin, who had taken over a senior role in his family's business, felt a huge amount of pressure to grow it to the next level. He was working hard and making great progress, but despite how much effort he was putting in, he still felt like he was failing. When we dived into it, we uncovered that these negative feelings were triggered by how much time he was spending on LinkedIn. During his daily scrolling, he'd constantly see competitors' stories about big work wins or posts about their clients' successes. That was creating a story in his head that everyone was winning but him, leading to huge feelings of being a failure and not good enough.

Sarah's workplace was organizing a sponsored run to raise money for charity and she desperately wanted to take part in it. Yet, despite her desire to get involved, she couldn't bring herself to even go out jogging, let alone sign up for the race. In our sessions, we uncovered that these ingrained fears were triggered by seeing how fast her colleagues were running. In her mind, if she couldn't keep up with or be as good as everyone else, then there was no point in even trying.

Finally, we have Corey. After a few setbacks in his business, he was feeling like a huge failure who would never amount to or achieve anything. All these feelings were built up and reinforced by Sunday dinners with his family, where he'd constantly hear how well his brother and sister were doing, how much money they were making, the holidays they were going on and how their lives were going.

Two important things to note here. First, as I mentioned above, each person's feelings of inadequacy and comparison were triggered by a specific external factor. Corey got triggered by his family dinners, Sarah by her co-worker's practice times, and Martin by his LinkedIn feed. But second, none of these people realized what was causing them to feel this way until they took the time to reflect on it. Because of that, they were oblivious to what was actually happening, causing them to think that there was something wrong with *themselves*.

With that in mind, the first step in giving up on comparison is understanding what *your* specific triggers are. Some of them may be situational—Sarah's trigger was only set off in the context of training for a race. Others may encompass your whole professional life, relationship, health or another large area of your life. Either way, you need to figure out whether there are specific situations, people or circumstances that trigger your negative feelings. Is it social media where you feel like you're missing out? Lunch with that old friend where you feel like you're behind everyone else? Someone getting recognition at work when you feel like you're not good enough? Seeing other people in better shape at the gym that triggers negative feelings about your body? This clarity is key, as the only way you are going to be able to break these thought patterns is to become aware of how and why they show up for you.

Another important note here: the reason you get triggered by these things may have roots in your past experiences—maybe even as far back as your childhood. When I met my client, Simon, he was doing pretty well in his career, and after years of dedication, he'd worked his way up the ladder and even secured a stake in the company. His hard work meant that he was able to afford a comfortable life for his wife and two kids, where they had four cars (including a brand-new Porsche) and lived in a six-bedroom house. The problem though was that despite how much he earned, he'd massively over-inflated his living expenses to the point that as quickly as money came in, it went out, leaving him and his family essentially living paycheck to paycheck. This was how he'd approached most of his adult life, and only as we discussed it did he uncover that growing up as the youngest of his siblings, he always felt overlooked and like he couldn't compete. These feelings were made even worse by the fact that his siblings had gone on to become doctors and rec-ognized professors—accomplishments that, just like his parents, made him really proud of his brothers. But often Simon felt like his parents used that success to benchmark his achievements, making him feel like he was always short of it and ultimately, causing him to resent his own choices and his brothers' success!

This internal comparison fuelled his need for validation, which he tried to fulfill by acquiring material goods, to show everyone else how he too, was doing great. And sure, that new car or pulling up to that big house may have given him some level of satisfaction. But through our conversations, it was clear that on a deeper level, they did nothing to make him feel better about himself. Especially with the added pressure of knowing that if anything went wrong, he could lose everything, as his expenses were so high. Despite that, for years he continued try-ing to fill the void by buying more and more, all in a desperate attempt to gain approval and impress those around him.

And he's not alone in behaving this way, as for many peo-ple, life has become a competition where they feel like they need to show off how well they're doing. This is why every year, they buy the latest phone, go on holidays they can't afford or live above their means building up debt—all to portray a life that in some cases, they may not even want or care about. All of this is often fuelled by feelings of inadequacy and wanting to feel like you're worthy.

This is why it's vital to gain clarity on why you think, feel and behave the way you do. With that in mind, take some time to figure out where and why these feelings come up for you, and whether your triggers are present-day occurrences or inter-nal struggles that go back many years. Because once you gain this clarity, that's when you can start breaking the control these triggers have over you.

Figuring out what you actually want

By now, you know how comparing yourself to other people can easily make you do things you don't want to do or buy things you don't actually want. But there's an important part of that tendency we haven't fully addressed yet.

Often the reason why you get stuck trying to get things other people have, is that you don't know what you want yourself! Think about it. If you were clear on what you wanted, then it would be far easier to look at what someone else has and say *"that's cool, but I don't actually want it—I want something else"*. Like in my earlier example, I had taken the steps to go out on my own and forge my own path by launching my business. What I hadn't done though was take the time to internalize and connect myself with my own goals. Even though I was making progress, I still felt behind my friends who were getting promotions, married and settled down. The problem was that I was looking at the whole thing through the wrong lens. I thought I was failing, as the indicators I was judging my success on simply weren't suitable for the path *I* was on.

To give up on comparing yourself to others, you need to get clear on what *you* want. There's an activity I do with all new clients to help them gain this clarity. To do it, close your eyes and imagine where you want to be and how you want your life to look like three months from now. Think about what *you* want to do for your career. What's important for *you* in your relationships? What do *you* want to be doing with your time? What do *you* want to look like? What do *you* want to happen in your life?

Once you've got a clear image in your mind, write a *vision statement* detailing everything about that picture. The reason why it's so important to write this down is because by getting it out of your head and down in front of you, it will start to feel real. Almost like a declaration to the world that this is the life you are committed to creating. Once you've written it down, what you do next is up to you. I've seen people keep it as a statement, others adding pictures to it or even turning it into a vision board. Personally, I use a combination, with motivational quotes, pictures of my family, photos of the house I want to live in, goals I want to achieve and people who inspire me.

The key thing after that is to then revisit this vision daily. Reading through it every morning will give you a conscious reminder of what you want. In turn, this allows you to focus and stay aligned with the choices you're making and remind you why you're making them. Not only will this be a great source of inspiration, but it can also be the push you need to show up and take action on the days you aren't feeling it, which will allow you to keep momentum and make sure you continue to move forward.

If you don't know what you want, there's a good chance you haven't put yourself in enough situations to figure it out or that you might have grown too comfortable in your current reality. That may mean that you need to start trying new things and putting yourself out there more, so you can learn what you enjoy and take in new points of view that could shape decisions around your future! So attend that class, do that course, or speak to that person who is doing what you think you may want to do. Whatever it is, start putting yourself in new situations to see what sparks your interest and happiness. Worst case, you hate it, and you can cross it off the list. Best case, you find something you enjoy and it's something you can add more of into your life.

Give yourself tunnel vision

Okay, you know what you want, and you know what triggers you to compare yourself to others. Now it's time to put the two together.

The key to solving this comparison-to-others problem is managing your focus. I like to think of it as creating tunnel vision, where you become so honed in on what you are doing that you prevent yourself from seeing the comparison triggers—they're not even in your field of vision anymore.

There are two ways to do this. First, you can eliminate or reduce your exposure to the triggers and situations that push you to compare yourself to others. This is especially useful for smaller triggers. For Martin, who we talked about above, this could be as simple as blocking his feed on LinkedIn. For Sarah, it could be choosing not to look at her colleagues' run times. Now I say *simple*, but I know that actions like this are not always easy, especially when they're bad habits that need to be broken. But if you know you have a particular trigger that you can avoid by simply making a change in your focus, your environment or your schedule, start there.

I used to struggle a lot with constantly checking social media and email. It was so frustrating, as I knew I shouldn't be jumping on it at every occasion, as I needed to give myself a break. The worst part is that I didn't even want to check it in the first place. Yet I seemed to always either give in, or do it without even thinking. I use social media and email for work almost constantly, so I couldn't just turn them off or remove them from my phone—which meant that any time I wanted to use my phone for personal reasons, it was almost impossible to resist checking email or opening LinkedIn. So I made an environment change: I got a second phone. Now I have a work phone that has email and social media on it, and a personal phone that doesn't. When I'm done working, I turn off the work phone, put it in a drawer and go into a different room. Then if I want to use my personal phone, I don't get tempted to check email or social apps—I couldn't even if I wanted to.

This can work for some larger triggers as well. If your past desire to compete has led to huge monthly expenses, then to take that pressure off yourself you may need to downgrade your lifestyle a bit. It's not the end of the world to let go of needing a new car or phone every year so that you can stop worrying about money in exchange. Or if your desire to prove your worth has led to working relentless hours at the expense of your family, then you may need to set better boundaries or cut down your hours so that you can slow down, find balance and enjoy life.

Other triggers, however, may not be that simple to avoid or remove. You probably don't want to stop spending time with that friend, skip family dinners or avoid speaking to your coworkers. Aside from triggering negative feelings, for the most part, these things are probably good for you and you definitely don't want to remove these from your life if they're bringing you joy and fulfillment.

This is where the second way to manage your focus comes in. Make a decision right here and now, that you are *simply going to give up on caring what everyone else is doing.* I know, I know. You're probably thinking that *"if it was that easy, Byron, I'd have done it already!"* But hear me out on this one, as I promise that it's far more doable than you think. Imagine your energy is a battery with 10 levels, where everything you put energy into depletes it one level. The battery recharges overnight, but once it hits zero, you don't have any more energy for that day. What most people do is put a lot of that energy into things that have nothing to do with their goals, priorities or what they want in life—like caring about what other people are doing. So if you start your day at 10 but immediately spend half an hour scrolling social media and feeling jealous of all the highlight reels there, you're already down to a nine. And let's face it, most of us do that a few times a day…so that might be half your energy right there. No wonder you're stressed and exhausted—comparing yourself to other people literally saps your energy without bringing you any closer to what you want!

The worst part, though, is that when the time comes to focus on what truly matters, you're out of bandwidth and don't have the energy left to follow through. Like when you know you need to hit the gym, work on your business or focus on your hobbies, but after a long day you're so tired you just sit on the couch mindlessly watching TV. Only then, you feel even worse, as you wasted all that time and did nothing to move your goals forward. A big part of the reason you feel exhausted is because you're wasting energy on people, situations and events that are not adding value to your life. By making the decision that I simply didn't care about what other people were doing anymore, I was able to shift that energy into my own life, creating a tunnel vision and lens of the world where I'm focused solely on my own goals and where I am going. When people ask me what my competitors are doing in business, I tell them honestly that I don't know. I've learned the hard way that I'd rather put my energy into my own work, instead of wasting it worrying about what other people are doing.

It's the same for social media. Even though I have built a large part of my business through these platforms, on a personal level I spend very little time on them. If anything, I'll maybe sign into my personal Facebook once every couple of weeks to check notifications, but I almost never scroll through the newsfeed. The reason is the same—I don't care what anyone else is doing. If it's a close friend I'll call or text them, or find out what they are up to when I meet with them. But for that old schoolmate going on holiday or the person cramming in another 6 AM run, I simply don't care, as it makes no difference to my life.

This is what giving up on comparing yourself to others is all about. And to be clear, it's not about being apathetic or indifferent. Instead, it's about deciding what is actually important to you, and then making a decision to not care about or waste energy on anything else. It means you can still be happy for the people around you achieving success, but their achievements and your own are no longer comparable in your eyes. And that, in itself, is empowering. When you choose to put your focus and energy into yourself, that's how you'll build and keep momentum.

But how do you stop caring?

While the decision to give up caring about what everyone else is doing and block out the world around you is incredibly empowering, I am also well aware that it is incredibly difficult. And unfortunately, there's no magical task or exercise to turn it around, and no feel-good quote to sum it up. Instead, it's a tough decision to make, and one you'll have to make over and over again until it becomes second nature.

Fortunately, something you gave up on earlier in this book will help you do that. Remember cause and effect? I wasn't kidding when I said it would apply to everything else you do. Comparing yourself to others throws you into a state of effect. And as I just mentioned, you'll find yourself back in that state from time to time. You will slip up. You will have moments you fall back into your old ways. You will still have times you feel like you're behind, not doing enough or that other people are better than you. And that's okay. Remember, this journey is not about eliminating your emotions or making you numb to the world around you. Instead, it's about recognizing when you fall into these thought patterns and putting yourself at cause so that you can break out of them as quickly as possible. When you catch yourself in that comparative train of thought, you need to shift your focus back onto your own goals and remind yourself that you don't care about what the other person is doing. This is how you can put yourself at cause and take responsibility for what you need to be focusing on instead.

It's not easy, and it may even require overcoming some other fears we've discussed in this book—like worrying about judgment and what other people will say or think. But you can either live your life worrying about everyone else, or you can give up caring and start living for yourself. You can't have it both ways. So I encourage you to make a decision about what's actually important in the life you want to live, and from today, start living it. Because when you give up on comparing yourself to others and their achievements, that's when you'll finally be able to build a life that you are happy with.

Part 3:

THE PEBBLES

I n the first part of this journey, you gave up on the two big things that keep you from getting started—reactivity and fear.

In the second part, you learned to give up on three smaller, but still significant, things that derail your progress and distract you from your journey—short-term thinking, fixating on the future and comparing yourself to others. Now, you're almost done with your toolkit to help you in the journey to the life you've always wanted to live. You've already given up on so many of the ways you sabotage yourself. You've made a ton of progress. You've gotten the boulders out of the way and taken the heavy midsize rocks out of your bag. The path ahead should be smooth sailing, right? Not quite.

There are two rocks left. They're the smallest—only pebbles. But they're not in your pack. *They're in your shoes*. And a pebble in your shoe can make even the clearest, smoothest, most scenic path painful to walk.

The two pebbles, one for each shoe, are *beating yourself up* and *putting off your happiness*. Both of them are here to distract you from how far you've come and how close you are to success.

So let's get them out of your shoes, so that you can finally start living the life you want.

CHAPTER 6

Maybe you should give up...
being so hard on yourself

———

I n this journey you've broken through many of the barriers that are getting in the way of you living the life you want to be living. But right about this point, a couple of things may be crossing your mind.

Firstly, you may be asking yourself why you had to give up on these things in the first place. Or even questioning if there is something wrong with you that caused you to have these challenges to begin with. You might even be wondering why you've not started this sooner, thinking "if only I'd known about this five/ten/twenty years ago, my life would be so much better now!" These thoughts and questions are normal. Once you start to make changes in your life, it's easy to look back and feel frustrated that you didn't act earlier or feel bad that you even behaved and accepted what you were doing before. That mentality in itself is a sign of growth, as it shows how far you've come. Remember, sometimes it takes hitting rock bottom or being in a painful situation for an extended period of time in order to be pushed to a point where you're ready to make a change. So sure, what you went through may have been frustrating and you're probably perceiving it as wasted time. But it was also necessary to get you to where you are today, as without it you may never have decided that you needed to give up on that way of living and turn it around. What you need to remember is that you can't change the past, and no amount of beating yourself up is going to undo what you did or didn't do. What you can do is focus on the present, and feel proud of the fact that you're here right now and you're pushing forward.

Secondly, you may also find yourself thinking that you've made *some* progress, sure, but you still have moments where you fall into the same traps. It can be so frustrating to still feel like you're taking one step forward and two steps back, especially after all the effort you've been putting in.

Again, the good news is that these thoughts are actually indications of progress. Because as you move forward, you start to create distance between who you are now and who you used to be. You also start to get closer to where you want to be. This, unfortunately, makes it all too easy to beat yourself up—either over where you were when you began, or how much more work you have to do to feel you've finished.

This is why the next thing to give up on is being so hard on yourself. While it's great to hold yourself to a higher standard and strive to be your best, being your own harshest critic almost always hurts you. If you constantly fixate on your shortcomings, missteps and failures, you can easily spiral into a state that constantly reinforces your low self-esteem, where no matter what you do, it will never feel like you are doing enough.

The truth is that you are making progress, learning lessons, and gradually (or even rapidly) improving your life. But if you haven't given up on being hard on yourself, you won't be able to see any of those good things. Instead, you'll be so focused on the few remaining negative parts of your life, that all the growing positive outcomes won't even register. It really is a lot like having a pebble in your shoe on a mountainside hike—until you take it out, instead of appreciating the incredible views, all you'll be able to focus on is how much your foot hurts.

Being too hard on yourself manifests in four major ways: trying to be perfect, dismissing your progress, judging your worth only by your success and taking criticism personally.

How they affect you and the way you need to handle giving up on every single one of them will be different. So let's look at each one in turn, so that you can break the cycle of being so hard on yourself.

Trying to be perfect

I completely get aiming to always do your best work. But there's a huge difference between doing your best and getting everything perfect. In fact, getting things perfect usually goes way beyond your best work and into unhealthy and obsessive territory. Think about it. If you do your best, you're probably going to be pretty happy with it, right? You'll have a clear sense that you've done everything you can and that the results are ones you can be proud of. But if you're trying to make things perfect, then you only see the holes in your best work...you see all the ways in which it is yet to be perfect. So you work harder. You put in more time, effort and energy. You come in earlier and stay later. You obsess over every detail. And most of all, you refuse to be finished. Every time you think you might be done, you also think that it needs one more pass, that it's not ready yet or wonder if you've missed something. So, you start tinkering and tweaking again. Meanwhile, weeks and months and even years are going by, and whatever you're working on never gets finished—or sometimes never even gets started.

One thing I've learned from working with my clients is that whenever someone tells me they're a perfectionist, or shows perfectionist tendencies in their life, it's usually a warning sign that something else is going on. And what's usually going on, is fear. I know, I know, we've already had a whole chapter on fear. And we're not going to just repeat everything from that chapter here. But it's worth pointing out that perfectionism is something many people use to hide from their fears of failure, success or judgment. After all, *"it's not perfect yet"* is a seemingly rational reason not to publish your book, start your business or post that video. It's so easy to convince ourselves that we need to get everything perfect before we take the step we really want to take…and thus never actually take it. So instead, we dabble, convincing ourselves that being perfect is a good thing, as when we finally get everything just right, it'll all be amazing and have been worthwhile. The thing is though, this is just a lie we tell ourselves to avoid facing what is actually going on inside our heads. Especially since it's far easier to tell yourself you're not yet ready or it's not the right time than it is to deal with the negative feelings of potentially failing or not being good enough.

And I'm speaking from experience on this one. My first book took 6 months longer than I'd planned because I wanted it to be perfect. Looking back, I can see that the reason I delayed was because I was so afraid that this crazy idea and vision I had was all going to come crashing down. I was worried my friends who said it wouldn't work would be right. That I'd let down my family, who supported and believed in me. That people wouldn't notice or care about what I had to say. So I kept pushing back the launch, convincing myself I needed to read it through and revise it *one more time* to make sure everything was perfect. It's only now that I can see how much I was getting in my own way. At the time I never even realized that my perfectionism was nothing more than a mask I was using to hide my fear.

It's also easy to use perfectionism as an excuse never to reach the life you want to live. Think about the journey you're on—you may well have climbed high enough on the mountain to have exactly the view you've been dreaming of for years. But because some little thing about it isn't what you consider perfect, you might think you have to climb higher than is safe, or turn back and try a completely different mountain instead—when in reality, where you are is well above those clouds already! Which is why if you're trying to get everything to be perfect, you'll never appreciate how good imperfection can be. This in itself raises the question of what even is *perfect*? Because here's the thing—*perfect* doesn't actually exist, and instead, it's an imaginary standard you've built up in your head that is simply unattainable. Because no matter how amazing you make or do something, there will always be room to have made it slightly better.

To defeat perfectionism, you have to get back in touch with what *doing your best work* looks and feels like—see just how good your *imperfect* really is. From there, you then need to figure out the outcome you want and set a clear expectation for yourself to stop working when you get to that point. Essentially, you first define what good looks like, and make a conscious choice to stop once you've reached it. A big part of this is recognizing that the extra time and effort won't lead to any further reward. Especially since not every project or task you take on needs to be a masterpiece. Instead, you'll often be in situations where it simply needs to be good enough to communicate a point or achieve a result. Like with that presentation you need to do at work to update everyone on the progress of a project. Sure, you could spend days improving it. But chances are you could also do it in a couple of hours and still get exactly the same outcome. Which is why all the extra effort is wasting time that could have been spent on making headway on something else. Now obviously that doesn't mean rushing, doing half a job or accepting sloppy results. This is still *your best* we're talking about here. But neither does it mean spending endless extra hours trying to make everything 1% better. Figure out what your best work looks like in whatever context you're in, and then *stop* once you get it there. Let your best be good enough. Chances are that it's probably exceeding expectations anyway.

With that in mind, whenever you find yourself worrying that something needs more work, you have to stop and be honest with yourself—is this actually not finished? Did I not already reach my goal? Have I really not done enough? Is there another reason why I'm pushing myself to do more? By taking the time to process what is going on, you'll be able to uncover whether something is truly missing, or if it's simply you being afraid to accept that you're done. This clarity will make it far easier to recognize when you are finished, which can then help you stop wasting more time and energy on something that isn't actually a problem.

I saw this recently in a client who was getting ready to launch a new product in his business. Yet instead of going live, he had convinced himself that the website wasn't fully done and needed refining. When we explored it further, it turned out he was merely unsure if he'd picked the right fonts and colors, so he'd been going back and forth on them for the last 24 hours. When we dived further into where the actual resistance was coming from, it turned out he was feeling paralyzed by fear. He'd put a huge amount of work into this new product and, understandably, he was worried about what would happen if it wasn't successful. That was the reason why he was trying to get things that didn't matter to be perfect, as it gave him a reason to postpone facing what could go wrong. It was only when he realized what the real reason for his perfectionism was, that he could see the true extent of his actions and hit launch.

This awareness is especially important in situations where you will never get it right straight away, like with a new project where you need to test, experiment and refine things along the way. In this kind of scenario, trying to have everything be perfect before moving forward isn't just frustrating, it's impossible. Especially since you will need to put it out there to see how people respond before you can improve what you have been doing. In this case, you delaying to get everything *just right* is getting in the way of the very action that will get you the clarity and results you want.

It's also helpful to think about what you are missing out on by holding back. So many people think being a perfectionist is a good thing, when in reality, it's the very thing stopping them from reaching their goals. That's why it's so important to start acknowledging the painful consequences of your delays. Whatever you are putting off, think about the growth you are losing, the time you are wasting or the progress you are sacrificing in the name of perfectionism. When you start to view perfectionism in this light, you'll be able to see it for what it truly is: sabotaging and holding yourself back.

When you take the pressure off yourself to get everything perfect immediately, you will open yourself up to a whole new perspective on what you *can* do. Instead of trying something new and immediately feeling defeated that you didn't get it right, you'll be able to enjoy the process of getting better. Rather than beating yourself up, you can view setbacks as either something you can be proud of, or simply another step in the journey.

Dismissing your progress

I know we've covered a lot so far. With the changes you've made and barriers you've overcome, you've pushed yourself to face your fears, let go of what you can't control and take steps towards the life you want. It's a lot to take in, and inevitably some areas of this book you will have found easier than others. Because of that, at times you may feel some internal frustration where you know what you should be doing, yet you're still not following through. Or maybe you're feeling discouraged because you know you've made a lot of progress, but there's still so much work left to do. And I get it. This journey will have many moments where you think you've almost reached the top of the mountain…only to realize you're still in the foothills. Talk about frustrating and discouraging. In those moments, it gets really easy to beat yourself up by focusing on everything going wrong or the areas you may not be progressing as quickly as you'd like. And the more you beat yourself up, the easier it is to quit. I wish I could tell you these moments won't happen for you, or that they'll be a piece of cake to overcome. But I hope you know by now that I'm not going to tell you something that isn't true, no matter how much you might want to hear it. Facing how far you have left to go will be a challenge. But there is a way to defeat the discouragement and downward spiral you'll be tempted to fall into when you face it.

Instead of looking forward, take a moment to look back. Allow yourself to see that the progress you have made so far, even if it feels small, is amazing. Each little step forward is taking you closer to where you want to be. Those small shifts are what will make you strong enough to face the challenge of moving forward, as they will be creating a foundation within you for making long-term progress toward the life you want. Think of it like a house you're building—one brick at a time. If you focus on how many bricks you have left to place, the whole project will be so intimidating that you might just quit. But if you look at how each brick you lay is growing the foundation and walls closer to completion, and you notice how many more you've laid since you started, you'll find a feeling of momentum and progress rather than anxiety and stagnation. Like that workout that pushes you to a point where you can't finish the very last set or minute. Rather than feeling bad about the fact that you're sweaty, out of breath and still carrying extra weight, focus on the fact that you faced it, gave it your all, and every time you will become a little bit faster. A little bit stronger. And a little bit closer to the level you want to be at. This way of thinking applies to everything you try to do or go for. Remember, you are on a journey here, not a race. So what if it takes a few extra weeks to get to where you want to be? Over the course of your life, does it really matter? A week or even a month or two may feel like a long time, but compared to a year or decade, it's nothing.

Now that doesn't mean being complacent, sinking back into your old ways or using that as an excuse not to push yourself. But it does mean approaching change with an open mind. Not everything will turn around overnight, and having to take time to work on it doesn't make you a failure. If anything, it shows how strong you truly are, as you're willing to persevere despite the uphill climb ahead of you.

With that in mind, make a point of regularly taking some time to reflect on what you've done to progress. Whether you want to keep a journal or record of your wins, or just take some time each week to think about where you were and how you moved forward. This simple action will go a long way in helping you connect to your journey, where even though you may still have a long way to go, you'll be able to recognize and feel proud of how far you've come.

Defining who you are based on your perceived success

When it comes to success and what you achieve in life, it's easy to allow your ambitions to become intertwined with how you see yourself. I see this all the time in my clients. When business is going badly, they take it as a reflection of themselves, like they're the failure, or they're not good enough. Yet when things are going well, they just expect it, dismissing good results as not a big deal. Or worse, they shift their focus to mistakes or what they could have done better, faster or smoother. And this way of thinking isn't just limited to your career or business—it applies to how you view yourself in every area of your life.

Here's the thing, though…*you are not your results*. That's not to say your progress or success isn't important. But at the end of the day, none of that has anything to do with your worth or value as a person. Seeing what you achieve as a perception of who you are is never going to lead to a happy and fulfilling life. If anything, it will lead to the exact opposite, especially since you will always be able to do better and there will always be another level to reach. I know it's hard to *not* do this. It can be difficult to separate yourself from your achievements, especially when those achievements are tied to an identity you've cultivated for yourself—entrepreneur, CEO, parent, spouse, athlete, etc. But if you want to be happy, you have to develop self-awareness on a deeper level to understand and define who you actually are. It's vital to know your values, what you stand for, what you believe, how you treat other people and what's important to you in life. These are the things that define you, not some trophies or ticked boxes to mark your accomplishments.

When you realize that the progress you've made and the challenges you've overcome don't have anything to do with who you are, it becomes so much easier to view your journey for what it is. So even if you do make mistakes, fall off track or don't move as quickly as you'd like, you can stop being as hard on yourself for what you did or didn't do. And this is key, because often in life you will never be able to control the outcomes of your efforts. You can give something your all, yet still come up short. Just take huge sporting events like the Olympics. Athletes dedicate their entire lives training for events and pushing themselves to reach their potential. But no matter how good they become, there is no certainty that they'll come out on top.

And it's the same for you in business, relationships or anything else you push yourself to get right. The only thing you can control is the actions you take. That's why, in the times you don't manage to achieve what you set yourself up to do, if you just focus on how you didn't win or what went wrong, of course you'll feel bad about yourself. But when you focus on the work you put in, how you showed up and the fact that you pushed yourself, then, even in the greatest defeats, you can still feel proud of what you did.

Taking criticism from others to heart

Remember in the last chapter we talked about creating a tunnel vision for yourself? A big component of that is to stop paying attention to a lot of the external influences and distractions in your life, the things that inherently trigger you into thinking you just aren't good enough. That's definitely still something you should do. But there's one loophole to that strategy that we have yet to address: your manufactured tunnel vision still allows a lot of people in your life; people who are more than just distractions. People you know. People you like. People you take advice from. People you don't *want* to tune out. And sometimes those people will tell you that what you're doing is wrong, misguided, problematic or doomed. We touched on this back at the beginning of the book, when we talked about why the world doesn't want you to give up on the things holding you back. With everything we are covering in this book and the journey you are going through, you will face some resistance along the way. It's inevitable. Some people won't understand the actions you're taking. Some will feel threatened by those actions. Some will even struggle to reconcile the results of those actions with their perception of you. Those people will often express those feelings by criticizing, shaming or attacking you for what you are doing. And because those actions are so important to you, it's really easy to take criticism around them as a personal attack on you, especially if the people are close to you!

Fortunately, you already know the solution to this problem. It's a variation of the solution to comparing yourself to others. Only instead of giving up on caring about what other people are *doing*, here you give up on caring what other people *think* about you.

Easier said than done? Sure. But also easier than you might think.

Here are three steps to get started:
1. Know yourself. When you are unclear on your values, goals, and priorities in life, it's easy to buy into other people's views and let them dictate the story you tell yourself. When you're crystal clear on who you are and what matters to you, what other people think stops mattering as much.
2. Remember that other people's thoughts and opinions are exactly that: *other people's thoughts and opinions*. They will only affect you if you allow them to do so. Even if one seems to be a real attack on you, you don't have to react defensively to it. Remember you don't have to stay at the effect of what other people think, and instead, you can put yourself at cause to change your response.
3. Ask yourself: is this person someone whose opinion I actually value or whose advice I truly trust? Note that this is not the same as being someone you love or someone you know loves you. If the answer is yes, then consider their thoughts and see what you can learn from them. But if the answer is no, then you have to block them out, recognize that what they say is irrelevant, and make a decision that you aren't going to allow their

opinion to influence how you feel about yourself—even if you still care about them.

These three steps will allow you to build and maintain the same kind of tunnel vision around criticism that you did around comparison, so you can either block it out or focus on what you need to learn from it.

Speaking of learning, not all criticism is a bad thing, and some may be a huge opportunity for you to grow. For instance, let's say you get feedback from a customer or your boss about where you could improve in your performance. Now, you can either dwell on the feedback, beating yourself up about how you aren't at the standard you'd like or need to be at or worrying about your job security. Or you can use the feedback as a sign of how you can improve, taking the learnings as a positive and viewing them as something you can focus on going forward. How you choose to look at the situation you're in will determine your feelings and perspective about what's going on—and impact how you're able to respond to criticism.

I had this come up with a client recently who was beating herself up because one of her managers told her that she hadn't done a good enough job in supporting her sales team. I pointed out to her that even if that was true, she *needed* to get that feedback in order to figure out what changes had to be made to keep her team accountable and support them in doing their best work. She literally would never have learned that lesson if her manager had just told her that everything was okay. Far from being a personal failure on her part, this experience was a massive learning point that will help her do her job much better going forward. This was even more important because she had never led a team before, making the responsibilities completely unknown territory. Because of that, diving in, making mistakes, getting feedback and learning from what happened was the only way she was going to improve. But she overlooked this at first because of the pressure she had placed on herself to get it all right straight away.

This is why it's so important to both recognize and embrace the fact that constructive feedback is coming from a positive place, where someone is simply doing their job of helping you improve. Even though it may be a sting to your ego, it's vital that you view this with the intention in which it was given. After all, no matter how great you are at something, there will always be room to improve. If the person criticizing you has your best interests in mind and is simply trying to help, then realizing that's the case, can make it far easier to take feedback for what it is and learn from it, instead of taking it to heart.

Once you get this right, you'll be able to have a whole new response to feedback. Instead of doubting yourself, you can either filter it out or use it as an opportunity to help you grow. If anything, it will also make you more inclined to ask for constructive feedback, as you'll start to view it as one of the quickest ways to improve.

The bigger picture

Beating yourself up is a hard habit to give up on. Even when you know how to better deal with it, it can still be easy to fall back into this trap whenever things don't turn out exactly the way you hope they will. And like most of the things this book is helping you give up on, it's okay if you don't get it completely right the first time. What's important is that you keep at it and make progress over time. You're on an ever-evolving journey, and you won't get to your destination overnight. There will be ups and downs and you will make mistakes along the way. That's simply part of the process and something that comes along with your growth. Creating that shift requires identifying where and how you beat yourself up, catching yourself in the act with negative self-talk and making a decision to give up on that state of mind. This comes from observing and understanding your inner monologue. When you are in that state of mind, you need to stop, mentally take a step back, and think about why you are feeling that way. What are you focusing on? And what do you need to do about it? Let's say you do make a huge mistake. You drop the ball at work on a customer's account and it's a pretty big disaster. In this situation, no amount of beating yourself up is going to undo the situation, and, if anything, dwelling on it is just going to make it worse. Especially since you are wasting time and energy that could be put into solving the problem.

Again, I'm not telling you to simply brush it off and become apathetic, but I want you to focus on what you *can* control. Because once you fix the mistake, then you can be proactive and uncover what went wrong, what you can learn from it and how to make sure it doesn't happen again in the future. You can see that a lot of this is down to perspective and how you choose to look at the situation you're in.

On a recent call, a client told me about how for the last few days, he got up early, finished all his work by 11 AM and then was able to spend some quality time with his wife who had a few days off from work. As he told me about what they did, he had a huge smile on his face, as it was the first time in two years that they had some time for just the two of them to connect and enjoy themselves. Yet within just a few moments, his focus shifted and he started talking about how guilty he felt for not using that time to work on growing his business. The smile dropped from his face and was replaced with a frustrated grimace. It was clear he was beating himself up for taking time away from his work. So I asked him why he started working with me. He thought for a moment, then said *"I needed help finding balance in my life. I've been working 16-hour days for years and it's killing me"*. As he said this, his face changed again, this time in realization. It was like the lightbulb went on in his head. Of course he was going to default to beating himself up for stepping away from work—he was taking action to give up on an unhealthy pattern of behavior, which his brain was fighting because it felt new and uncomfortable. In fact, he had made a conscious decision to work less and spend more time with his wife that week! And he was only being hard on himself for making that decision because it was an action out of the ordinary.

This is the kind of self-awareness that's vital to develop around being hard on yourself. And it comes from you knowing what you want, being conscious of the choices you make and allowing yourself the time to work through and figure it out. When you learn to do this consistently, you can pinpoint where those harsh thoughts are coming from and start replacing them with more compassionate ones.

And that's the second key to giving up on being so hard on yourself: compassion. It takes time to change years of hard-wired patterns and reactions, and trying to rush the process or get it right immediately is just going to make you feel worse about what you are doing. In reality, the fact that you're working on turning things around is amazing in itself. Developing compassion for yourself helps you focus on the bricks you've already placed, rather than the ones you haven't gotten to yet.

Along a similar line, between your goals, ambitions, family, health and other commitments, you are probably doing and taking on far more than you realize. This is why as uncomfortable as it may feel, it's okay at times to cut yourself some slack. That doesn't mean you aren't moving forward or are being lazy. But it does mean that you are starting to accept yourself for who you are and give yourself the space and recovery time you need. Something that seems like a big deal today—like taking a night off to rest, only feels that way because you are looking at it as an isolated event. When you look at it over the course of a week or year though, suddenly it doesn't seem so bad. Especially if you recognize that after a few days of pushing yourself, you need that night off to recover and re-energize for the rest of the week. Meaning *not* giving yourself that break is actually short-sighted and likely to cause further problems in the future. The balance you need to find here is being able to be truthful with yourself. You have to be able to make a conscious decision about what you need (like choosing to spend the evening relaxing at home, after weeks of working overtime) instead of simply using it as an excuse to avoid what you need to do (like skipping your workout again because you had a long day).

The truth is, you may never get to a point where you completely stop being hard on yourself. And that's okay. You need an element of that internal drive to keep pushing yourself to improve and move forward. The difference is recognizing when those feelings are unjustified or having a negative effect. After all, you're not a robot—you will make mistakes, you will need to recharge and you will need all of that to grow. That doesn't mean you're a failure or that you aren't any good. Those setbacks simply show that you're making progress, as you're putting yourself in situations where you can evolve. The way you make the distinction though is through compassion, where you are honest with yourself; where you are able to identify when you did your best and view that as the win. In many ways, this perspective will allow you to make the outcome irrelevant! And in the times you didn't give it your all, you can use that as motivation to do better next time. This is why compassion is the mindset that will allow you to give up on being so hard on yourself. It will enable you to embrace the journey for what it is, giving you a whole new perspective on your progress and how you are doing.

CHAPTER 7

Maybe you should give up...
putting off your happiness

D uring our time together, we've spoken a lot about where you are going, what you want and what you need to do to achieve your goals. Because that's ultimately why we're here—to help you get out of your own way so that you can finally take control of your life. All of that raises a bigger question though—why do you want to live the life you want to live? There's no right or wrong answer here, and every single person is going to have their own answer to that question. If you boil it down, the core reason for all of us is that we want to be happy.

Regardless of the specifics of your desires, you will want your life to be joyful and fulfilling. You will want freedom and to be able to spend your days enjoying your time. You will want to think, feel and do things that make you smile. And by extension, you will want to stop doing all the things that cause you pain or stop you from reaching happiness. Happiness is a great ultimate goal. But have you ever noticed that no matter how happy you want to be, you never seem to get there?

There's always some reason or excuse not to be happy. Maybe your results weren't quite as good as you'd hoped. Maybe you only had a few moments to feel happy before you had to go put out another fire at work or deal with a cranky kid. Maybe you're looking down on yourself and don't think you deserve to feel happy right now, so you put it off until a later time. Except later never comes. Every time you want to be happy, you find another reason not to be, and another, and another after that, leaving you stuck in a vicious cycle where essentially you're delaying your happiness indefinitely. So no matter how happy you want to be, you never actually feel that joy.

This is the last thing you need to give up on. The final pebble in your shoe that's keeping you focused on the pain of moving forward or how far you still need to go, instead of how far you've come on this journey. That's why, to fully take control of your life, you need to give up on putting off your happiness. Because if you're not happy, then what's the point in everything else?

Why not be happy now?

Putting off happiness is the most counterintuitive matter in this book. The reality is, you can be happy right now if you want to. Even if your life is terrible or you're struggling with a lot of different problems, you can probably find a few things to be happy about. And as you make progress on this journey towards the life you want and gradually give up on more of the things that are holding you back, you will find even more reasons to be happy.

When you think about it like that, being happy should be easy. But for most of us, being happy is one of the hardest things to do. In my work, I've found four main reasons people struggle to be happy—or at least to be happy *now*.

First, we're busy. It's easy to get stuck in a cycle where whatever is going on in the moment seems more important than something you know will make you happy. There's always someone asking for your attention. There's always something else you still need to do, another responsibility to fulfill. After a long day, your happiness almost becomes an inconvenience— one more thing on your never-ending to-do list, where instead of bringing you joy, it becomes just another stressor in your life.

When I started working with Sam, he wanted to get back into archery, but he found himself having time scheduling conflicts. At work, he was senior management—and almost every day there was a new problem that needed his attention. Sam used to love archery as a hobby when he was younger. But despite wanting to make it part of his routine as an adult, he just couldn't get the time to get to the archery range. So he'd push it to tomorrow. Then next week. Then next month. Before long, archery became just another thing he wanted to do, but despite his good intentions, never got around to it. He felt terrible—he desperately wanted to restart this sport he enjoyed so much, but he felt like he just couldn't make it happen. He put off his happiness in favor of work. Now, that's something we've all done. It might not be archery, but we all give away our happiness for things that feel more important in the moment. I know that life is busy. You have commitments and responsibilities and you can't simply drop them all. But life is always going to be busy. There are always going to be challenges and setbacks, or things that feel more important right now. That's why the perfect time to be happy is never going to come. If you want to make it happen, then it has to become a priority, and you commit to making it happen—no matter how busy you are.

Second, we put other people's happiness ahead of our own. Many of us have an ingrained tendency to go above and beyond for others, yet feel guilty for doing something for ourselves—almost like our own happiness isn't as important. This is a trait I see in pretty much everyone I've worked with, where they have no issue bending over backwards for other people or tending to their needs, yet when it comes to their own wants and desires, they always take a back seat. This pattern of behavior can create a mental barrier where you become so used to putting everyone else first, that just the thought of doing something for yourself can make you feel guilty.

I had a conversation with a client who faced a huge inner battle. Mary was thinking of taking a regular night off where she'd get her husband to look after the kids while she went to a fitness class and then relaxed with a hot bath. On the outside, these seemed like very simple actions. But because she'd spent years seeing herself as the caregiver for her husband and kids, even taking one night a week for herself felt selfish to her. Don't get me wrong, I have huge admiration for the desire to help and look after others, and I'm sure that you are doing it with the right intentions. But putting everyone else's happiness first usually means you never get around to your own. This can cause resentment, where after a while, prioritizing everyone else's needs above your own causes a huge amount of frustration and pushes you even further away from truly being happy.

While Mary thought she was being selfish for wanting an evening of self-care, once she spoke to her husband, he encouraged her to do it. In fact, he welcomed looking after the kids and giving her the space she needed to recharge mentally. This again shows how easy it is to be your own worst enemy, where you accept how things are instead of the help you need. The reality is that the people around you who love you want to *say yes to you*. They want you to be happy, they want to support you and won't think of you as greedy for needing respite or a night off. You can't expect them to guess what you need though, which is why you have to tell them.

Third, we confuse happiness with positivity. It's easy to think of happiness as manifesting through smiles, being unphased by what the world throws at you and seeing silver linings in the worst of situations. But this kind of idea often places unnecessary pressure on people. After all, you are always going to have bad days, moments when you are challenged or times when life pushes you to your limit. That's why you don't need to be in a constant state of positivity and excitement to be happy. Instead, you need to learn to take the good with the bad, so that even on your worst days, you are still content with who you are and what you are doing. That's how you build a fulfilling life.

As much as they may hurt or you wish they didn't happen, you need the less-than-ideal times to happen too–they keep everything else in perspective. Because if life was great all the time, then the good times wouldn't mean as much. This way of thinking allows you to find happiness in even your darkest moments. Despite things going wrong and you feeling far from positive, you still feel happy for what you have. That's the difference. And it's why it's so important to recognize that happiness, and the feelings that come with it, aren't related to constantly feeling great, positive or everything going right.

Finally, we make our happiness dependent on achieving a particular result. We've talked about this a bit already, but it's worth repeating. How many times have you told yourself *as soon as X happens* or *as soon as you get through Y* then you'll be happy? But then once you get to that point, you realize you aren't—or at least not as happy as you thought you'd be?

Next thing you know, you move on to the next goal or milestone, telling yourself again that once you reach it, that's when you'll reach happiness. The whole cycle starts all over again. Before you know it, you're spending your life constantly in pursuit of what you want next, telling yourself that next goal, that next threshold, that next milestone will be what you were missing all along. The problem is that there will always be another level to reach. Another raise to earn. Another client to gain. Another pound to lose. As soon as you get close to what you think you want, the goal post will move.

On the other side, there are people who struggle to even get started. If you're in this category, you spend all your time thinking about what you want to achieve, creating fancy vision boards and getting excited about how your new life will look and feel. Yet despite how much you want it, you never actually take the action needed to get there. I think, to a certain extent, we are all guilty of this in one way or another. We talk or think about what we want and how amazing life will be when we get there, only we never get started with our life plan to begin with. The thing is though, by putting off taking action, you are putting off being happy—while also giving yourself a handy excuse for why you aren't happy. Either way, when you make your happiness depend on reaching a goal, you are putting it off indefinitely.

What is happiness anyway?

These reasons we put off happiness help us understand a lot about what happiness isn't. It's not fitting everything perfectly into your schedule. It's not necessarily being the caretaker of everyone else in your life. It's not just being cheerful and positive. And it's not reaching a goal (or even thinking about one).

So what is it, then? As with all of these issues, if you ask a dozen different people, you'll probably get a dozen different answers. But here's the answer that's come to me after the last several years of working with people who want to stop putting off their happiness: *Happiness is being the best version of yourself that you can be right now.*

There are three things I really like about this definition. The first one is that it's actionable. It's not some oversimplified, flowery proverb about how happiness comes from within. Statements like that aren't wrong exactly, but they are misguided. Happiness is not something you achieve, it's a state of mind that comes from how you view, engage and approach life. It's not that happiness is deep inside you, it's that you find happiness when you find what you really want—which is another way of describing taking action to be the best version of yourself in the present moment.

The second is that it's something you can do *now*. It's not something you have to wait to do until you get all your work done or you take care of everyone else. It's not getting into a more positive mindset or hitting your next milestone. It's not even being the best version of yourself that you could ever be. It's being the best version that you can be in this very moment. That small difference frees you from the need to put off being happy until later.

And the third thing I love about this definition is that it grows with you. Wherever you are on your journey, you can find happiness—which means there's no longer any reason to treat happiness as something that only comes as the end result. Instead, you can find happiness in every moment along the way, from the most fulfilling successes to the toughest struggles. It's like pushing yourself to train for an upcoming race or taking a chance to start your dream business. Both of these will have huge challenges, and the process will inevitably have setbacks, problems, emotional swings and moments you fear you will fail. Yet overcoming those challenges also brings some of the most meaningful moments into your life. This is why you need the lowest lows to be able to fully feel and embrace the highest highs and the journey in between. Where you know that you gave it your all, went for what you wanted and pushed yourself to see who you could become.

Being the best person you can be in a given moment will make you happy because happiness is tied to identity. Think about the times in your life you've felt the happiest. I bet during those moments you also really felt like yourself—secure, authentic, aligned, *right*. So how do you do this? What does it take to be the best version of yourself right now, so you can give up on putting off happiness until later? Unfortunately, the answer does not lie in simply giving up on everything weighing you down and holding you back. While that still needs to happen, on its own, it's insufficient. I've seen it in my clients time and time again. It's really challenging to accept that you can be happy as an effect of dropping all those boulders, rocks and pebbles along the way. To find happiness in the now, we need a more goal-oriented approach.

Three steps to happiness now

Here are three practices that will help you be the best version of yourself right now.

1. Prioritize yourself

Remember Mary, who struggled to put herself first because she was trying to take care of her family 100% of the time? Here's another piece of her story: she was *really* struggling just to maintain her day-to-day equilibrium. Between her career, family and daily responsibilities, she was burned out and exhausted. Because of that, Mary had been pushed to a point where all the frantic rushing around would leave her on edge and she'd often get frustrated or snap at her kids. And this just made her feel worse about herself, as she knew that reaction was out of alignment with the mother she wanted to be. In turn, she'd then feel like she had to do even more or try even harder to make up for how she behaved.

That's the problem when you don't make time for yourself. Neglecting yourself actually makes it harder to deal with the never-ending problems that life throws your way. Without joy, relaxation or recovery in your life, you can easily end up in situations where you wonder what's the actual point of all of the stress and aggravation you are putting yourself through. Or where you feel even more mentally and emotionally drained, to the point that everything feels like a far bigger battle than it should be. In other words, it's impossible to be the best version of yourself in this moment (or any moment) if you're struggling just to get through the day. It's also much harder to give up on reactivity, fear, comparison and the other issues discussed in this book when you're exhausted, stressed, frazzled or burned out.

Even though it may feel uncomfortable or go against every fiber of your being, you need to practice putting yourself first at least some of the time. How you do that is completely up to you. You could sign up for a class you always wanted to try. Go for a walk that helps you clear your mind. Hire a babysitter to have date night on Thursdays back on your calendar. Take that weekend fishing trip. Go to a concert to see a band you love. Schedule an afternoon off to relax with a movie. It doesn't matter, as long as it's something you enjoy. Just figure out whatever it is that you need to do to recover, relax and rejuvenate yourself, then don't put it off. Do it this week. And then do it again next week, and the next, and so on.

Prioritizing your self-care like this does three things. First, it allows you to experience happiness now rather than as something that can only come later. Second, it gets you in the habit of treating yourself as the best version of yourself—someone who not only deserves to be happy, but actively does things to make themselves happy. And third, it allows you to feel more energized and engaged with the rest of your life, including your job, your relationships and those who need you.

All of this is also going to go a long way toward improving your feelings of self-worth. After all, when you prioritize yourself, you mentally reinforce the idea that you are worthwhile and deserve to be happy. I know that following through with this may feel uncomfortable or even selfish. But really, if putting yourself last burns you out to the point of being the worst version of yourself, doesn't it make sense that putting yourself first will help you become the best you? And when you are able to show up more energized, more engaged, less stressed and more present, how much better is life going to be for you and those around you? So if anything, isn't it selfish *not* to put yourself first once in a while?

2. Get to know the best version of yourself

A big reason why most people never reach their goals is because they spend too much time focusing on what they want without thinking about *who* they need to become to make it happen. This creates a disconnect between your desires and your identity, which leads to feelings of futility and frustration. If the current version of you could never achieve that goal, then who is *the you* who will?

So the next step here is to figure out what the version of you who can achieve your goals looks like, and start pushing yourself to show up as that version of yourself in everything you do. The good news is you've already gained that clarity in a previous chapter of this book. Remember where I tasked you with visualizing who you want to become, to act as a conscious reminder of where you are going and why? That person is pretty close to the version of yourself who's achieved all your goals. All that's missing is how they did it.

Using the clarity you gained on how you want your life to look, you need to figure out what the future version of you did to make that life a reality. Think about what habits, behaviors, and non-negotiable parts of their day they followed through with to get them to where they are. Did they put aside time each day to work on their business? Were they consistent with putting out those videos? Did they make it to the gym even if they were tired? Did they have a proper morning routine to help them ease into the day? Did they prioritize date night to feel connected to their partner?

There are no doubt going to be numerous actions they took that allowed them to get to where they are. Especially when you look at their life holistically and factor in everything from their health to their career and their relationships. That's why thinking about this now will show you exactly who you need to become and what behaviors you need to embody to create the life that you want. You will know the standards you need to hold yourself to if you want to look back on your days knowing you lived them as the best version of yourself.

This awareness also acts as a great reminder in times when you don't feel like taking action. Let's say after a long day you're tired and want nothing more than to binge-watch Netflix on the couch. With that in mind, what would that future version of you who has reached their goals have done at this moment? Would they have made excuses and put it off? Or would they have pushed themselves regardless of how they felt? This works because rather than just focusing on what you don't feel like doing, you can shift your focus to how those moments of consistent action will get you to where you want to be.

You can also use this clarity in times you face challenges in your life. Let's say you and your partner feel disconnected or are having problems. Think of the future version of you who has the relationship you want. What are they doing that you're not? Regardless of the problem, by looking ahead to the future version of yourself, you'll be able to figure out what you need to do to change your situation.

When you start living, thinking and acting in this way, you'll see a huge surge of momentum starting to build in your life. Aligning your goals with who you need to become will not only push you to move forward, it will also allow you to look back with a sense of pride, knowing that what you did was true to the best version of yourself. (It's important to note that this version of you will evolve over time as you move through your journey. That's why I highly encourage you to repeat this exercise every 90 days!)

3. Be present

One of the overarching themes of this book is how the things you need to give up on keep you from living in the moment. And as you've gone through the journey of gradually giving up on each of those burdens, you've probably noticed that it's starting to get easier to be present in a given moment. Now it's time to take that one step further by getting you to intentionally become present in everything that you do.

I had something happen in my life recently which was a reminder about why this is so important. One Wednesday morning while I was writing the first draft of this book, I saw my dog Harvey was struggling to move. He's an older dog and I assumed he'd hurt his back jumping off the couch, as he'd done that several times before. Regardless, I rushed him to the vet, as he was struggling to stand and he kept falling over. It turned out that he had a stroke that morning, causing him to lose the ability to move anything below his neck, and all feeling in his left side. The vet essentially gave us two options: we could either put him to sleep then and there, or we could take him home to spend a bit more time with him first. Either way, what she said was that Harvey's time had come. As the words came out of her mouth, my emotions completely took over. I went all lightheaded and dizzy, and I had to sit on the floor as I felt like I was about to faint. If you're a pet owner, then you'll probably relate to the feeling that your pet is like your child. For me, it felt like my entire world was caving in. I just couldn't comprehend what was happening, especially since earlier that day everything was fine. Now, Harvey wasn't in any pain, so we decided that there was no way we were giving up on him yet. Over the next few days, he started to slowly recover, regaining some strength and his ability to stand and walk. We started doing physio and rehab on him, and four weeks later as I write this, he's made pretty much a full recovery. Sure, he has a slight limp, but apart from that, he's back to his old self.

This experience gave me a huge wake-up call as to how, out of nowhere, life can come crashing down. This realization has given me a whole new appreciation for enjoying the little things in life and being present in every moment. Even small things like taking Harvey out of our apartment to go to the toilet now feel precious. Just being there with him, seeing the sky, feeling the breeze and being aware of my surroundings brings so much joy. Especially knowing how close we came to that being taken away.

When was the last time you stopped to think about the fact that you're alive? That you're living, breathing, that you have this chance to see another day? When you realize how amazing the fact that you are here right now actually is, life's problems suddenly don't seem so bad. And sure, even though so many things may be going wrong, there are probably also a ton of things going right. You don't need your world to be turned upside down to start thinking and feeling this way. Instead, you just need to make a conscious decision to bring yourself into more moments, where instead of living life on autopilot, you become aware of what you're doing.

The secret to being happy is being present in everything you do—whether that's working, spending time with your family, hitting a workout, or even something mundane like washing the dishes. Rather than allowing life to happen to you or getting lost in your thoughts, you need to pull your focus into the moment. This is how you feel connected, engaged and present. How you feel *more* of life. How time no longer feels like it's just passing you by. And how you find happiness *now*, not at some indefinite later point.

Why we need happiness now

There's a fantastic book called *The Top Five Regrets of the Dying* where a hospice nurse, Bronnie Ware, recorded what people coming to the end of their life wished they had done differently. In her findings she found the top five regrets were:

1. Not having the courage to live a life true to themselves, instead of the life others expected of them.
2. Working so hard.
3. Not having the courage to express their feelings.
4. Not staying in touch with old friends.
5. Not letting themselves be happier.

Numbers one through four are hugely impactful, and I bet you can find some parallels within them to things you want to give up on. But the fifth one hits me the hardest. These people lived out their entire lives putting off their happiness. And it was only when they were facing their mortality that they realized what they'd been doing—when it was too late to do anything differently.

Do you know what hurts far more than failure? Than rejection? Than not getting it right? Regret. I don't want that fate for you. That's the real reason I wrote this book—I don't want you to wake up at 65 or 85 or 105 and look back at your life regretting what you didn't do. I don't want you to be facing the end of your life and still be putting off your happiness.

So I'm going to finish this last chapter with one more strategy for giving up on putting off happiness: *remember it's not too late.* Yes, we all have a limited time on this planet, which is why I'd encourage you to start your journey of giving up on the things holding you back right away! But I'll also give you the flip side of that: just because you don't know how much time you have left, doesn't mean you're already too late to start. So many people avoid making changes or taking what they perceive as risks because they feel it's too late. Like a 35-year-old being scared to change careers or start their business as they're already comfortable in their job. Or the 60-year-old worrying it's too late to get in shape. Sure, this may have been true in 1930 when life expectancy was 58. But in this day and age with all the advances in medicine, there's a good chance you'll hit 90, 100 or even more! Meaning you have far more time than you realize. Yes, life may be short, but it's also the longest thing you'll ever do. So, until death comes knocking at your door, don't count yourself out! You still have a lot of days and opportunities to make the most of.

I saw a quote online recently which perfectly sums this up. To paraphrase, if you're worried about starting because you'll be a certain age when you finish, you're going to be that age anyway, so you may as well be doing what you want when you get there. This perspective is so powerful, as it's a stark reminder of the journey that is life. Yet so many people overlook this, convincing themselves the game is over, when actually, they're only in the second half.

The reality is that you are never more than one decision away from a completely different life. This is why when it comes to finding happiness, the best advice I can give you is also the simplest. Figure out what matters most to you in life and what brings you joy, then make a decision that every day you are going to prioritize doing the best you can to move towards it. Don't set yourself up for a life-long regret. Give up on putting off your happiness by being the best version of yourself you can be and live life with intention right now.

NEXT STEPS

You made it! Through this journey you've uncovered exactly what you need to give up on to take control of the life you want. Despite the awareness and growth that you've created, it's important to realize that as you change and evolve, you will still encounter resistance going forward. You will have moments where you're at the effect of the world around you, where life happens to you and it controls the way you think, feel, behave and react.

You will have moments where your fears keep you stuck in your own head, as you get pulled into mental stories or doubt yourself. You will have times where you get stuck in short-term thinking, fixating on the future or comparing yourself to other people. And you will still have moments where you are hard on yourself, or where despite your best intentions, you allow life to get in the way and you put off your happiness.

And that's okay! You will have times where you stumble or fall off track. We all do. The difference now, and where the real growth comes in, is how you recognize these patterns and behaviors. Instead of allowing them to hold you back, you can become aware of when you're getting in your own way. You can stop, process how you feel, put the situation into perspective and take back control. You can give up on everything that is standing in the way of you becoming who you are meant to be.

I'm so excited for you and can't wait to see what's next in your journey!

Byron Morrison

WATCH THE VIDEO SERIES

To help you take the next step in your journey, I've created a short video series to ensure that you keep moving forward. In these videos, you'll gain clarity on who you need to become to take your life to the next level. I'll also help discover what's standing in your way and the exact actions you need to take to get to where you want to be. You'll then be able to use all of the tools from this book to get out of your own way, so you can take control of the life you deserve.

This video series is free and it's my gift to you for making it this far.

You can watch it on demand at:

www.byronmorrison.com/bonuses

JOIN THE COMMUNITY

I f you haven't already, make sure you join the Facebook group. This is going to be your go-to place to share your progress, make friends, get support, and keep yourself accountable. I'll also be in the group answering questions, sharing content and giving you further resources to help you on your journey.

You can join the community at:

www.facebook.com/groups/maybeyoushouldgiveup

GOING BEYOND THIS BOOK

know that we've covered a lot in our time together and it's a huge amount to process and take in. That's why if you want to take this to the next level, I created the **BREAKTHROUGH** course.

In this course, you'll discover how to get clear on your goals, upgrade your identity and uncover exactly what life on your terms looks like. I'll show you how to get out of your own head, break through beliefs that are holding you back and help you stop spending your days in a reactive state. You'll also develop the right routines, build your intuition and get the tools you need to deal with stress, procrastination and overwhelm.

I'll take you through everything you need in easy-to-follow videos. That way you can approach the journey in your own time and at your own pace. I'll also show you how to quickly and easily implement these changes in your life, taking all of the guesswork out of the process, so that you can just focus on becoming the best version of yourself.

By the end, not only will you feel more in control, you'll change the way you think, process problems and deal with setbacks. You'll feel more confident, have clarity on what you want, where you're going and you'll be able to show up as your best in everything you do. Putting you back in control, so that you can take your life to the next level.

As a thank you for reading this book, I've put together a special offer. You can find out more and get started at **www. byronmorrison.com/breakthrough**

THANK YOU!

just want to say a huge thank you for taking the time to read this book. I hope you enjoyed reading it as much as I enjoyed writing it.

As an author on a mission to make the world a better place, I can't spread this message on my own. Because of that, it would mean the world to me if you took a moment to leave a review for this book on Amazon, so that more people like you can give up on what is holding them back and take control of their lives.

When you have, drop me an email at **byron@byronmorrison.com** and I'll send you an exclusive bonus not available anywhere else as a thank you.

You can also connect with me and follow more of my content online by searching for Byron Morrison on Facebook, Instagram, LinkedIn and TikTok.

Thanks again and I look forward to meeting you and following your journey in the community.

Byron

ABOUT THE AUTHOR

Byron Morrison is a bestselling author, mindset and performance coach, specializing in helping people get out of their own way and take control of their lives. For the last decade, he has worked with CEOs, entrepreneurs and business leaders from around the world, helping them to reach their full potential. His books and work have been featured on TV, in magazines, as well as promoted on radio shows and podcasts globally.

You can find out more about his other books and courses at: **www.byronmorrison.com**

To discuss booking him for speaking engagements or events get in contact at: **byron@byronmorrison.com**

ACKNOWLEDGMENTS

Firstly I want to say a huge thank you to Jules for continuing to support and push me on turning this crazy dream into reality. I never would have gotten this far without all your help and support. Also thank you for editing my books, helping with my marketing and bouncing around business ideas.

To my parents, who, without their support and guidance, I never would have become the man I am today. Thank you for believing in me and giving me everything I needed to get to where I am.

To James Ranson and David Hancock for helping bring this book to life.

I also want to say thank you to every single person who has supported me on this journey. Whether you've read my books, watched my videos or shared my message, from the bottom of my heart, it means the world.

And finally, to you, for taking the time to read this book. I hope you enjoyed going through it as much as I enjoyed writing it. I look forward to our paths crossing again in the future.

A free ebook edition is available with the purchase of this book.

To claim your free ebook edition:

1. Visit MorganJamesBOGO.com
2. Sign your name CLEARLY in the space
3. Complete the form and submit a photo of the entire copyright page
4. You or your friend can download the ebook to your preferred device

Print & Digital Together Forever.

Snap a photo   Free ebook   Read anywhere

CPSIA information can be obtained
at www.ICGtesting.com
Printed in the USA
JSHW021547250623
43719JS00001B/2